TEACHING LIFE SKILLS TO CHILDREN

A Practical Guide For Parents And Teachers

Dale R. Olen

Paulist Press ◆ New York ◆ New Jersey

To my Dad and Mom, who taught me by living;
to Joelyn, my partner in trying to teach our kids;
to my children Andy and Amy, hoping they learn
the skills of living

Library of Congress
Catalog Card Number: 83-62954

ISBN: 0-8091-2618-4

Published by Paulist Press
545 Island Road, Ramsey, N.J. 07446

Printed and bound in the
United States of America

Contents

Introduction   1

Skills for the Children

1. Helping Children Like Themselves   5

2. Practical Steps on Enhancing Self-Esteem   18

3. Teaching Children the Rhythm of Communication   27

4. Receiving: The Skill of Listening   34

5. Giving: The Skill of Sending Direct Messages   40

6. Teaching Children to Believe
    and Think Realistically   49

7. Leading Children Toward Responsible Behavior   61

8. Helping Children Engage Life Fully   77

9. Promoting Children's Decision-Making Skills   88

10. Teaching Children Religious and Moral Values   94

11. Encouraging Children Toward Healthy
    Sexual Attitudes   101

12. The Skill of Loving and Contemplating   112

Contents

Skills for the Parents-Teachers

13. Making the Transition from Authority
    to Consultant   119

14. Managing Feelings and Behaviors   127

15. Modeling a Full Human Life   139

Introduction

When I became a parent, at the same moment I became a teacher. Four years later, when our son, Andy, went to a cooperative pre-school three afternoons a week, I realized that his mom and I were not to be his only formal teachers. From then on, my son would be taught a variety of things by people I did not even know.

As I realized that I must teach him how to live fully in this world, I was in awe of my responsibility. Likewise, when I recognized that many other adults would also attempt to teach him how to live successfully, I was scared. Who were these people? What did they believe? What did they think was important to learn?

While these questions have plagued me every year, a larger question has always loomed in me. When my kids grow up and have finished with their school room teachers and their at home parent-teachers, what skills do I hope they have? Beyond classroom abilities, what skills for living life fully do I wish for them?

The answers to that question make up this book. I write to parents and teachers because together our mutual responsibility is to help our children gain the personal and interpersonal skills to engage life to its richest degree.

It most likely helps us as busy parents to have some idea of what skills are most helpful to our children. And, as teachers, it might help you to know the skills we parents seek to impart to our children. In this way, we can hopefully work together to attain what is best for the children—an ability to navigate through life in a loving, free and happy manner.

Whether consciously or not, parents and teachers attempt to impart skills for living to their children. The more explicit we

1

can be about what those skills are and how they can be taught, the more likely we will teach them. Furthermore, if both parents and teachers know the skills, chances for systematic collaboration between the two groups is increased greatly. I want to encourage parent-teacher associations, in particular, to work together in identifying these life skills and cooperating through discussion and programs in teaching life skills to our children.

A note to teachers. Most of the examples used in this book are between *parents* and their children because I know those best. Please adapt the principles and techniques to your experience with children in the classroom.

Skills for the Children

Chapter 1

Helping Children Like Themselves

Recently, a man came to see me. Forty-four years old, he stood 5'8" tall and weighed 295 pounds. Herbert disliked himself intensely. He described his dislike as a giant ball with jagged edges that sat in the pit of his stomach. The ball was rotten, smelly, and evil. He believed that he never did anything right. He wanted desperately to be close to someone but was convinced that "nobody could ever love me."

Herbert had never married. He was a most generous and kind man. He could anticipate people's needs and enjoyed responding to them. He possessed an excellent sense of humor and people responded to him in a very positive manner. If his friends knew he did not like himself, they would be surprised because they certainly liked him.

How did Herbert develop such a negative view of himself? Did anything happen to him when he was a youngster that could now so strongly influence his life?

Well, psychologists have presented many answers to these questions, and no single theory seems to explain the whole issue. I want to share with you some answers that I think might help you understand this most important issue.

Answer 1

Herbert goes through four mental steps to view himself negatively. He started this process when he was a child and continues it today.

An event took place. He accidently knocks over a flower pot and breaks it. Mom reacts by yelling: "What's the matter with you, Herbie? You're so clumsy and irresponsible. Go right up to your room!" Herbert goes. The four steps Herbert goes through in his mind are:

1. Perception
2. Self-Talk
3. Judgment
4. Reaction

First, he *perceives* or takes in what happened. He observes the facts of the case. Assuming his perception is accurate, he took in:

fact 1—He knocked down a plant.
fact 2—It broke.
fact 3—A mess was created.
fact 4—His mother became angry.
fact 5—His mother said he was clumsy and irresponsible and wondered what was the matter with him.
fact 6—She wanted him to go to his room.

Second, Herbert *talks to himself* about what he perceived.

"I wonder if Mom doesn't like me anymore. Maybe I am very irresponsible. If she thinks I'm clumsy, maybe I'll never be any good in sports. Maybe I'm not really clumsy, but just had an accident. Then maybe Mom is wrong about calling me clumsy."

This is self-talk. Herbert considers his perceptions of reality, and then raises hypotheses about what they mean. He rushes through his mind possible interpretations of the event in order to know how to respond.

Clearly, Herbert, at age 8, did not consciously think through all the "maybes" suggested above. His self-talk occurred in a split second. He laid out all the options available to him at the moment and quickly moved to the next step, *judgment.*

Third, Herbert *judges* his hypotheses and decides what his perception of the event means. This judgment step stands as the pivotal moment in positive and negative self-esteem. If he judges positively he concludes: "Mother is simply irritated with me and so uses those words; but it does not mean I *am* a clumsy and uncoordinated person. In fact, I know from being on the basketball team that I am quite coordinated."

On the other hand, if Herbert judges negatively, he concludes: "She really dislikes me and that must mean I am a bad boy. I am a clumsy ox who can't do anything right."

Again, it is important to note that children do not think out a situation in their mind this thoroughly or slowly. The process speeds along so that their self-talk and judgment may elude their awareness. Yet these steps have taken place.

Now, you ask, why do some kids make positive judgments and some, like Herbert, negative ones? The range of answers to that question will, in part, be answered below. However, for now I can say that the child who judges positively has *experienced* acceptance as a person from the significant people in his or her life. Children who judge negatively have not experienced that acceptance unconditionally. They have sensed (not consciously thought, but felt through their body) that somehow their goodness as persons was based on a set of conditions outside of themselves. More on this later.

Young children can learn to make certain judgments that will cause considerable difficulty for them in later life. They learn to believe such things as:

I am a good person when I please my parents.
I am a good person when I am successful.
If I make a mistake, I am a failure.
If I don't accomplish this task or goal, it is (I am) terrible.
If Dad or Mom is upset, it is my fault and I am bad.
I should excel in this sport; if I don't I am inadequate.
If you don't pay attention to me, then I don't count.

These kinds of conclusions, reached early in a child's life, play havoc on self-esteem. Generally, the types of judgments that lead to negative self-esteem include:

Dramatic Judgments: It's awful; She'll never like me again; I can't stand it in this house; They are the worst parents in the world; I can't do anything right, etc.

Demand Judgments: I must get straight A's on my report card; My parents shouldn't be so strict; I have to have a date for the prom; I gotta make the team; I absolutely need that bike; My teacher shouldn't treat me unfairly, etc.

Self-Blame or Inclusive Judgments: I got a B on my report card, therefore, I am dumb; I have acne, therefore, I am ugly; I'm afraid to ride the roller coaster, therefore, I'm a chicken; No one is talking to me at this party, therefore, I must be a real drip, etc.

You can see that Self-Blame judgments are the ones that ultimately sabotage a child's feelings about self. Dramatic and Demand judgments set the stage for a clinching Self-Blame statement. For example, "I must get straight A's (Demand judgment), and if I don't I am dumb (Self-Blame judgment)." "I have to make the team (Demand); if I don't I'll die (Dramatic), and I probably won't make the team because I'm no good anyway (Self-Blame)."

Fourth, after Herbert judges his perceptions, he *reacts*. He has concluded to his inadequacy as a person, so his reaction is depression. He feels down. The reactions from a judgment can be a behavior and/or a feeling.

Let's say Beth judges herself as incapable of being successful at most anything. When cheerleading tryouts come up, her *reactions*, based on her judgment of self, will be:

Behavior: she won't even try out.
Emotion: sadness because she is left out again.

Hopefully, you can now see the dynamic whereby children and adults develop their self-esteem. First, they *perceive* an event; second, they *talk* to themselves about what it might mean; third, they judge what it does mean; fourth, they react according to their judgment.

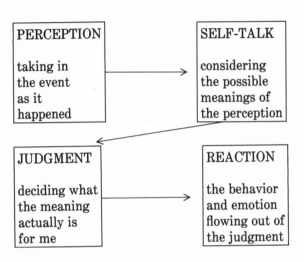

The critical step is the *Judgment*, what a child decides the event means for him or her. If you are to do any work in helping your child value himself or herself, the point of attack is the child's judgments about self.

Answer 2

To understand why all children don't make positive judgments about themselves, a brief explanation of the positions a child takes toward life will be helpful. I am indebted to the theory of Transactional Analysis in explaining this reality.

Herbert is born and immediately assumes a psychological position. He experiences himself as helpless and without any power to direct his own life. He experiences his parents as all-powerful and the source of all that leads to Herbert's happiness—food, warmth, protection, comfort. His parents are OK; Herbert is not OK. He views himself in relation to the world as less than or as inferior to other people. Rooted in him now is the *experience*, not the judgment, of his own inadequacy. So you see, his parents already have quite a task in helping Herbert to like himself. His *experience* is contrary to feeling good about himself. Even though he cannot make judgments yet, he already leans toward the negative side.

This position is called "I'm not OK; you are OK." Here lies the soil in which the seeds of negative self-esteem are sown. If Herbert's earliest experience continues, the belief that he is not OK and his parents are OK intensifies.

The way you respond to the new-born child will determine whether or not the child will continue to believe "I am not OK; you are OK." If you tend to be overly protective, you tell your child that he or she cannot do anything on his or her own. Such children become fearful of trying anything because they believe that they cannot do it right without Dad or Mom helping out.

If you tend to rescue your child from frustrations, you again reinforce the child's belief that he or she is incapable of anything without parental help. "They are OK; I am not."

Another way in which your child can remain stuck in "I'm not OK; you are OK" occurs when you criticize the child rather than the behavior. Saying "How dumb can you be?" when Susy puts her head through the screen teaches her that she is dumb—not OK. And you must be OK because you are judging her as less than yourself. (More on this later.)

Some children develop another psychological position—"I'm not OK, and neither are you OK." This seems to begin around age seven months when the child starts creeping. Now this little person experiences some independence and some power. She can do something for herself. She continues, however, to look to Dad and Mom for help and to satisfy her needs. But they abandon her by not holding her as much as before, not talking to her as frequently, and, in general, by not giving her a sufficient dosage of attention. As the child gets older and is lost in the middle of a six-child family, maybe she feels left out by her parents. If she does, she may easily conclude "I'm not OK; you are not OK either."

This position holds a great deal of pessimism and futility for the child. The ultimate result, in the most severe cases, is suicide. "I can't help me and neither can anyone else. What's the use?"

A third position occurs when the child is not simply abandoned, but abused. If the child experiences physical or psychological abuse, he may well learn: "You are certainly not OK, and the only time it (or life) is OK (or I am OK) is when I am alone, protected and safe from those terrible people."

The child is safe and OK when he is placed in his crib and no longer needs to endure the violence of the parents. That violence may be physical, or it may be more subtle, but just as violent. Parents who did not want their child may communicate that belief more powerfully than we might think. Parents may indicate to one child that he is disdained by them in a variety of ways. The end result is that the child believes: "I'm OK; it's the rest of the world that is not OK."

The ultimate result here, in the most severe cases, is murder. "Why kill myself? I'll kill you because you're no good anyway."

Finally, the fourth possible position is "I am OK; you are OK." Of course, this is what we want for our children. If the child gradually experiences some independence and some power in his or her own life, and yet feels continued love and support from Mom and Dad, that child will have a good chance of learning: "Hey, I'm not so bad myself; and neither are they." The child senses personal power; he explores his world, he takes some control over it; he can navigate in it and it cooperates in return. He realizes: "I *am* OK, and so are you."

Staying with your child in a supportive and accepting way most effectively develops a position of "I'm OK; you're OK." If the child experiences abandonment or an overly protective, stifling response from the parent, he may remain in an "I'm not OK; you are OK" position. So the trick is to balance allowing the child his or her independence and self-empowerment, while at the same time supporting and accepting the child as is.

Answer 3

In our culture, self-esteem and a sense of meaning in life are closely linked. If you have a purpose for living, for getting up in the morning, then you have self-esteem. We develop that meaning based on three pillars or sources. We may look to our work (or the productive use of our time) for meaning; we may center on our interpersonal relations for meaning; and we might turn to God or some kind of deity for our purpose in life. (Fig. 1)

If during our lifetime one or more of these pillars is shaken or broken down, our sense of meaning and our self-esteem may be severely tested. A man loses his job and the important pillar of work crumbles from under him. If he has placed much of his sense of worth on his work, you can see the problem that might arise. The same is true for the man or woman who loses a most significant relationship by reason of death, divorce or breakup in friendship. These are critical times in a person's life and the stuff of "mid-life crisis."

MEANING IN LIFE SELF-ESTEEM				
W O R K		INTERPERSONAL RELATIONSHIPS		**G O D**

When an adult over-focuses on any of these pillars, he or she will be in trouble. If a man bases his esteem and value so fully in his work that the other pillars suffer, he is heading for trouble when that work is taken from him by poor health, age, or boredom. The woman who places her entire sense of worth in her relationships as a mother is heading for difficulty when the children grow up and leave home. The college student, so fully involved in the "Jesus Movement," who abandons his studies (work pillar) and friends (relation pillar) for God may well find that when the emotional response to God wanes, so may his sense of worth and meaning.

The point of all this is that these pillars and the importance we place on them are developed in childhood. Children learn to value certain things as important. For example, Steve might come to believe that "winning is everything." If he wins "Candyland" as a three year old he feels good; if he loses he storms and feels awful. Later, he doesn't mind playing a bit dirty to win at basketball, or cheating a little to end up with more marbles than anyone else. When he wins or is successful, his folks rave about him and to him; when he loses they seem more crushed than he. This boy is learning to build up his pillar of *work* as the source of his worth and value as a person.

Our society reinforces the child's belief that doing things successfully makes you worthwhile. Oftentimes in therapy and in psychological testing the first question I ask is "Who are you?" About eighty percent of the time the person will first say: "I am a salesman or a housewife or a student, etc." They tell me what they *do* when I ask who they *are*.

"Achieve, be successful, win"—these are the passwords in American society that easily reinforce the belief that "my value is based on what I *do*." Self-worth then becomes based on status—a physician has more value than an electrician, and a woman executive more worth than "just a housewife."

In childhood, it is easy to believe that the captain of the cheerleaders has more value than the flute player in the band, and the A student is "better than" the C student.

Jimmy hits a home run and a parent says "Good boy." Achievement equals goodness. Jenny washes the car and Dad says "You're really a wonderful kid." Doing and being are married as one in the children's minds. They are now set up for the fall of Humpty Dumpty when in later life their job or position is taken away or they fail to succeed at some task. Their self-esteem crashes.

The same thing can happen if a child learns that "I am worthwhile only if others need me, or like me, or are with me." Teenagers often express to me their conclusion that "the most popular kids are better than I am." Somehow *having* relationships means *being* better.

The difficulty here lies in a child's belief that "I am OK when others are valuing me or attending to me." If a child places too much emphasis on this pillar, then when he or she is alone or has experienced some rejection, the child "goes to pieces." "Life is no longer worth living," which translates to mean "I am no longer worthwhile."

Finally, the pillar of God can be focused upon too exclusively. This rarely happens in early childhood, except in those instances where the parents or teachers claim "God's disappointment" with a child's behavior. In this ploy parents project their own disappointment, and they use God to bolster their position in the situation.

Teens may focus too exclusively on the God-pillar for a sense of meaning and purpose. This occurs when a child's sense of stability and security is shaken in some way. The child then grabs on to the one reality he or she feels will not change or abandon him or her—a transcendent, spiritual force—God. By fully involving themselves in religion some children discover security and meaning in life, and experience themselves, often for the first time, as being worthwhile.

Unfortunately, for many of these children, the emotional high of this religious experience wanes, just as it does in a boy-girl relationship. When that happens and the teenagers no longer *feel* close to God, their self-worth may come crashing down. At that point the best thing we can do for them is to simply *be* there. Our being there immediately affirms the pillar of relationships. Upon that pillar (us) they can then begin to rebuild their self-worth.

Answer 4

I'd like to offer you one more answer that has become increasingly important to my understanding of a child's self-esteem. It involves a very subtle belief, learned in early childhood, and operating in most adult lives.

Kids learn early in life: "Two realities, if they differ, cannot stand side by side. One of them must go."

Let me explain. Sandy is six years old. She goes to bed on school nights at 8:00 P.M. Tonight she crawls into bed at 8:00 and Dad sits down to read a book. At 9:00 Sandy appears at the bottom of the staircase and calls "Daaaaady." She is trying to present to him her reality.

Dad jumps right in and says: "What are you doing up at this hour, young lady? You get up those stairs and get to sleep. It's way past your bedtime." He has presented his reality.

So Sandy has her reality and Dad has his. As we will see they are very different.

Sandy tries again: "But Daddy, I . . ."

Dad interrupts: "No buts about it. You have school tomorrow and you have to have your sleep. So get up there this instant."

She goes back upstairs.

Now, Sandy's reality was that she had become sick and thrown up in her bed. Dad's reality was for her to be in bed sleeping. These two worlds differed. And Sandy learned a most powerful belief: "When my world differs with Dad's world (or perhaps with anybody else's world), my world doesn't count." Or more profoundly "I don't count."

Think of all the times when your children's worlds might not seem to count for them. Your child falls and scrapes her knee. She cries and you say, "It's OK." Your world differs from hers, since clearly her scraped knee is not OK for her. Or your four year old keeps insisting, as mine does, "Daddy, Daddy, Daddy," while you're talking to your spouse. You say, "Joe, quiet. I'm talking to your Mom." But maybe you never get back to him. He experiences his world as not counting. Or your teenager likes loud music that you don't like. You insist on quiet music. His experience? He doesn't count.

I am not suggesting that, therefore, you should give in to your child's world every time it differs from your own. I am saying that through many of these experiences your child learns this subtle but powerful belief: "My world does not count when it differs from Dad and Mom's world." And some kids translate that even further to: "*I* don't count when other people differ from me."

This belief radically influences a child's self-worth in times of conflict and differences. If the child's world is not understood (you don't have to agree with the child's world to understand it), then the child can easily draw the conclusion: "I do not exist for them."

Two responses come from that realization. The child feels *hurt* and accepts the conclusion that he or she does not exist. This results in poor self-esteem. Or the child struggles harder to show Dad and Mom that he or she does in fact exist. The child then reacts with *anger*, and yells back, demanding, in effect, that the folks pay attention and notice that the child really does exist. A child's anger is almost always an effective way of getting the parents to deal with him or her. It gets the child the experience of existence. "See, I do exist."

When my son was five years old he hit me in the back of the head with a belt one night while I was helping my daughter get her pajamas on. With irritation I asked: "Why in the world did you do that?" Immediately he said, "So you'd pay me some attention." His world and mine had differed. He wanted me to focus on him. I was focusing on my daughter Amy. One of our realities had to change. He could have sat back and felt hurt and jealous because I wasn't matched up with his world, or he could demand that I attend to his world, which is what he did in a rather dramatic, although inappropriate way.

You see, my son Andy believes that two opposing or differing worlds cannot exist side by side. One has to go. Because he fears that his world will have to go (that he won't exist for me) he reacts strongly and attacks my world to force me to change and correspond to his world. He hits me in the head with a belt.

You might be wondering, "What else could kids believe when they experience two differing worlds?" An alternative belief much more reasonable and sound is, "Two differing worlds can, in fact, stand side by side psychologically, and *both* be legitimate or valid." Practically, both worlds cannot always operate at the same time, as when your son and you might want the car at the same time. But even though a decision for action must be made, it can be done in a manner that does not "invalidate" the other person's world.

How to work concretely with the dynamics of your children's self-esteem will be discussed in the next chapter. So far I have only focused on how those self-concepts develop. The next chapter should make considerably more sense to you now that you have attended to the growth and destruction of self-worth.

Chapter 2

Practical Steps on Enhancing Self-Esteem

All right. Now let me try to be as concrete and practical as possible. How might you help your children grow in positive self-valuing?

1. Acknowledge and Try Hard To Understand Your Child's World

More than anything else you can do, accepting your child's world as real and valid enhances his or her self-esteem. Adults, as well as kids, tend to feel good about themselves when someone is attending to them. I used to really enjoy talking with a classmate of mine in graduate school because I found him so interesting. On reflection, I realized that he always seemed very interested in my views and thoughts. He attended to me and I felt valued.

Kids are the same. They may not be cognitively aware that you are attending to them, and that you consider their world valuable, but they experience it. You might not be able to listen to your son immediately when he demands your attention while you're talking to someone else, but you can let him know you'll attend to him as soon as you finish your present conversation. Then when it is over, make sure you ask him: "What did you want, David?"

Attending to a child's world, her beliefs, feelings, values and behaviors tells that child that she is OK just as she is. When your child says: "Mommy, I hate you," and you recognize that child's negative feelings toward you, you say to her in effect: "Mary, I know you're upset with me right now, and it's OK to be so. Having that strong feeling is neither good nor bad. It's just there."

Listening skills come to play here. When you receive any message your child gives you without immediately judging it, you are letting that child know: "Al, *you* are very important to me and whatever you think or feel I'd like to share because I value you."

Al may, at times, express his world in loud and crude ways, or in confused and reluctant styles, or jokingly or casually or sarcastically or sadly. If you can stay with him in his manner of expression and follow him as he takes you on this trip through his mind, you will do much to help him build positive self-esteem. Just stay with him. Agreeing or disagreeing is for later on. If you jump too quickly to judgments, Al's experience will be, "You don't care about what I believe. You only care about yourself."

2. Compliment and Criticize Only Your Child's Behavior, Not the Child

This suggestion helps to offset the belief that what children *do* equals who they are. Johnny is not a "good boy" because he got all A's on his report card. He is a good boy period, who happened to get all A's. Mary is not a bad girl when she disobeys her mother. She is, in fact, a good girl who is disobeying.

Try to detach your child's behavior from the person, and then respond to the behavior. If Timmy did a good job of brushing his teeth, you say: "Timmy, you sure got all those teeth tonight." You acknowledge what he did. You don't judge him to be a good person because he did it.

Alice is not a "dummy" because she threw a rock through the window. She made a poor judgment and you don't like the consequences of her act, but that does not make her dumb. Oftentimes, our negative statements about our children are camouflaged in a sharp question, such as, "How dumb can you be?" by which we mean "You certainly are dumb!"

You might be thinking "What difference does this really make? My child doesn't make the distinction when I criticize her behavior and not her." You are probably right that she does not make the intellectual distinction, "Oh yes, my parents are criticizing my behavior, but clearly not me." This distinction actually has more immediate impact on the parents than the child. If you are very aware of viewing your children's behaviors as distinct from who they are, then you will *always* be valuing the children no matter what they do or don't do. And if you possess that spirit, your children will experience it from you. You will communicate your valuing of them because your whole orientation will be geared toward the children as good human beings independent of what they do.

Fortunately, there is a time to address the children in their being. When they are *doing* nothing, I would encourage you to go up to your children and say something like: "Tammy, you know what? I think you're a really neat kid." Or "Tammy, I really love you." Or "Tammy, I sure value who you are."

Now, young children will often accept such a statement, and even return a like statement. Older children, especially if they have not been used to hearing such things, will probably react negatively or in an embarrassed way: "Aw Mom, cut it out. That's so dumb." Don't feel badly if that happens. Your child simply doesn't know what to do with your expression. The best thing you can do is simply receive your child's discomfort and let her know again that you think she's neat. You might say: "Jenny, I know that sounds sort of dumb to you, but I mean it. I think you're a neat kid."

A week or so later you might do it again. "Hey, Jenny, I know you might think this is goofy for me to say, but I love you." A little teasing sense of humor here can go a long way. After you say it, you might rush out of the room while she's lying on the couch. But she's been getting the message, and that's the important piece. And the message is: "Independently of anything you do or don't do, I value you as a good person." That message is most helpful.

3. Accept the Fact That Kids Are Kids

This may sound fairly straightforward and obvious, but, in fact, parents often find it difficult to let kids be kids. Our expectations of children rocket forward when they reach the age of two and a half. Until then we allow them to be infant-kids. It may annoy us at times when they whine and spill milk, but we usually don't yell at them or discipline them in any way. We expect tiny tots to whine and spill milk. But, when they reach three, we expect all of that behavior to stop and for them to "grow up." (By the way, saying "grow up" to our children is a great way to help put them down.)

Once children are able to talk and understand our talk, we expect them to function in a rational and reasonable manner. We expect them to respond to life situations as an adult would. You can observe this expectation within yourself whenever you notice yourself saying: "I can't believe he did that."

Six year old Peter is discovered by his mother in the living room with his sand toys, Tonka truck and all. The rubber tree is out of its giant pot and Peter is excavating the plant holder. All the dirt lies spread out upon the new bright yellow carpet. It's a mess. Most parents would initially react in an upset manner. Understandable. Peter "knew" he wasn't to play in the living room. Any rational adult would *know* that you don't play "excavation of plants" on the new, bright, yellow, expensive carpet. And Peter, who is six, should know better, we think. He should know how to think as an adult. *But he doesn't know how to think as an adult.* He is a child growing up. And kids growing up have significant lapses of rational thought. They regress at times to infant-like thinking and behaviors. That's why we often say things like "You are acting like a two year old."

Children fluctuate. That's what makes them so fascinating, challenging, and frustrating. Just when we think they're growing up and able to be trusted in making some decisions, they regress and do something that startles us. The teenager who uses the car in a responsible manner calls you from the police station and says the police stopped her because she had a carload of kids who were drinking beer. Surprise. "That's just not like Becky," you say. "I don't understand her."

That may not be the way Becky normally functions, but it is how kids growing up behave at times. Children of all ages gradually behave in more rational ways, but all along the journey they have moments of regression. When they do regress, they behave with the judgments and reactions of much younger children. That surprises us and often initiates our frustration.

Kids are kids. They will regress to earlier childhood. The more we realize that fact, the more accepting of the child we will be. And accepting the child as "a-person-on-a-journey-to-grow-up" will do much to allow the child to also accept him or herself.

4. Attend to and Encourage the Process of Your Children's Lives Rather Than the Content

The content of a child's life consists of the things he or she does. Examples of content are:

1. the number of points he scored in the game
2. the grades she got on her report card
3. the amount of money earned from the paper route
4. having eaten all her vegetables
5. having a large number of friends
6. knowing how to ride a two-wheel bike
7. talking in full sentences
8. being able to add and subtract
9. getting her driver's license

The *content* is the end result—the successes and failures, the victories and defeats. The *process* is the personal quality or style the children bring to the content.

I hope you can see the difference. The old adage might help here: "It's not if you win or lose, but how you play the game that is important." A child can get a straight A report card and behave as if she were Ms. Brilliance. Or, she can accept the grades in a graceful way as a human measure of her intellectual capacity and her diligence. The process is much more significant than the content. We are helpful to our children's sense of worth by highlighting the processes of their life rather than their successes and failures.

Every human being, and therefore every child, displays qualities of goodness and lifefullness. One child might show considerable empathy toward other children; another might demonstrate real perseverance in doing a task; another might display an inquisitive mind. These qualities come from within the child and make up the "stuff" of the child. This is, in part, *who* the child is. Making the team or eating all his food does not make Freddy to be Freddy. However, as mentioned earlier, our society tends to equate who a person *is* with what he or she has accomplished. Society's belief is, "Freddy *is* his content."

The more we can work away from this belief, the more we help our children hold onto their own worth whether they scored twenty points or sat on the bench throughout the entire game.

Susy complains: "I can't do anything right," when she drops her baton in the parade. That's a statement about content. She has not succeeded. Based on that failing experience, she makes a statement about her person: "*I* can't *do* anything right." It is an easy next step for a child to say: "Therefore, I am a failure." She has focused on the content of her life and drawn a negative conclusion about herself.

Her parents can now attempt to focus on the process of her life instead of the content. The parents observed Susy's exuberance while marching in the parade. She walked with a bounce in her step, a broad smile on her face. She winked at little kids sitting on the curb, and she even waved while twirling. People felt lightened when she passed by. The dropped baton makes little difference; the quality of lifefulness Susy presented spoke volumes about the kind of person she is.

So her parents might say to her: "Susy, I know you feel sad about dropping that baton." Remember. First you want to *receive* your child's feeling no matter what it is. Then a little later you might go back to Susy and comment: "You know, darling, something I really value about you is how much joy and life flows out of you. For example, this morning in the parade, I could see how much joy you gave to people along the route by your smile and waving. That's really neat."

See what I mean? You acknowledge your child's feelings because she's focused on the content; but then you highlight for her a lifeful process she employs and you let her know that's what you value.

I find it a helpful exercise at times (when my children are fast asleep!) to think about and identify those processes or qualities my children employ that enhance life. Identifying these qualities helps me focus on them. The more I focus on them, the more likely I will express them to my children. The more I express them to the children, the more likely they will value these qualities and use them as an accurate basis for their own self-esteem. They are good persons because they possess life-giving qualities, not because they have done well or poorly at some task.

5. *Teach Your Children That Their Experience Is Valid Even If It Differs from Others' Experiences*

As discussed in the previous chapter, a most subtle and powerful belief our children develop is, "If your world and mine differ, one of ours is invalid and must go." If children invalidate their own reality they will feel inferior, hurt and overly-sensitive. If they invalidate the other person's world, they will feel angry, aggressive and superior to others. Both responses are signs of poor self-esteem.

What you want to work toward with your children is a realization that in differences both worlds are valid and, in fact, do exist. In other words, a high degree of tolerance for differences is the goal, and a belief that if someone differs with me it does not mean that he or she is attacking my person or vice versa.

How do you help your children attain that kind of tolerance for difference? Your ability to *model* tolerance of differences will best serve your children's tolerance development. In a two-parent family the most effective modeling takes place between you and your spouse. If you can share your differences directly, honestly, in a non-attacking manner, and if you can receive your spouse's reality in an understanding and non-threatened manner you will graphically demonstrate for your children a respect for and tolerance of each other's world.

Modeling is the first line of attack. It is also the second line of attack. When you and your children have differences, your ability to respect and value your own and your children's world speaks loudly to them about accepting differences.

Specifically, you best achieve that result by receiving your children's world in a non-judging way. To understand your children's world is to acknowledge that it exists and is valid even if it differs from your own.

A prerequisite to acknowledging and understanding your children's world is that as a parent you slow *down* your responses to your children. Most of us respond so quickly to our children's world by sharing ours immediately. They then conclude that we did not understand them and that their world does not count for much. So before sharing your world with them, try, try, try to slow yourself down and first hear and acknowledge your children's view of reality. You don't need to agree. You do want to notice it and affirm that it and the children exist. You do want to show them that you respect their world.

6. A Little Technique with Older Children in Building Self-Esteem

If you have a child over eight, who seems to have low self-esteem, but with whom you can talk, I want to share a process I often use in counseling with young people. It is based on the conviction that a child's behavior and feelings toward self spring from his or her *beliefs* and *thoughts* about self. (Chapter 6 will focus on this topic more fully.)

The technique goes like this:

You ask your child: "If you could be any way you wanted to be what would you choose?" A teenager could respond to this question. Younger children (8–11 years) might need a question like, "If you could be like any other person, who would you be like?" They might say Pete Rose or Batman or the Hulk. Then you can ask, "What about that person do you especially like?" That way you get to the quality.

Let's say you ask the teenager, Joan, what she'd like to be like. She says, "I want to be popular."

You ask: "What would it take to be popular?"

Joan: "I'd have to be friendly and outgoing."

You: "If you think about people who are friendly and outgoing, what do you guess they would have to think like? What would they have to tell themselves?"

Joan: "Well, such a person would have to think, 'I am a likable person'; "I am kind'; 'There are people who have liked me when they got to know me'; 'The sooner someone knows me, the faster they will like me.'"

You: "What would the person need to think for her to let herself be known faster?"

Joan: "'I won't probably get hurt or rejected if I share myself with other kids'; 'Most kids like it when people share with them.'"

Now Joan is starting to get thoughts in her head that support positive action. You can try to point out to her that she can have these thoughts if she wants to. It's only her thoughts that keep her from what she wants. Then encourage her to practice these new thoughts and to try to behave according to the new thinking. Finally, keep checking up on how she's doing. Try to continually encourage the kind of thinking that leads to behavior she likes in herself.

The whole thrust of this technique is to help a child learn how to change his or her perceptions and thoughts so as to change behavior that is more satisfying and fulfilling. This technique takes considerable work and patience because you're helping your child change a way of thinking. But with steady work, a young child can change his or her view and belief and thus enhance esteem of self.

Chapter 3

Teaching Children
the Rhythm of Communication

Clearly a child's ability to communicate stands as the foundation of all the skills of living. The philosopher Gabriel Marcel observed long ago that the first learning of the new-born child is not simply "I am," but "We are; therefore, I am." Children and adults experience themselves in *relationships*. And relationships are established through communication.

If all the skills and values of life were laid out before me as a parent, and I were given the choice to select one and impart it in its entirety to my children, I would choose the skill of communication. More than any other skill, I would want for my children the ability to create the rhythm of giving and receiving with whomever they met. If they were good receivers, not only would their sensitivity and tolerance heal and enhance other lives, but their openness would allow them to drink in the world and enrich their minds and hearts. Were they capable givers, others would come to know them well and value them, which in turn would support my children's sense of well-being.

I still remember a professor of mine in college stating: "If a college student wants to make it through school and graduate with good grades, intellect is not the most critical factor. The student will do it by his or her ability to communicate effectively." I agree.

You can help your children develop this skill most effectively by your willingness to *receive* them and *give* to them your own inner richness. That's communicating with them. Then, as much as possible, spend time with each child talking and talking and listening and listening. Yes, the children may "drive you crazy" at times with their incessant chatter and questions, but hang in there with them, because you are aiding them in the most central skill for a happy life.

Finally, you can help them by teaching them to read and write. Certainly, you need to start this while they are still young. Read to them and read to them. I know it gets boring when they always want the same book read over again. But motivate yourself at that time by saying: "I'm teaching her to communicate. And this is the greatest gift and legacy I can give her."

Teaching the Rhythm of Giving and Receiving

What I am about to tell you is clearly the single most important thing you will ever hear about communication—be it with your child or any other living person. It stands as the most fundamental principle in communication, and if you get it, your ability to teach your children to communicate will improve markedly.

The message is this: **In order to have effective communication you must always have a GIVER and a RECEIVER.**

That's it. Overwhelming, isn't it? Certainly it is so simple and easily stated, but the impact of this meager realization can literally transform personal relationships.

You see, oftentimes this Giving–Receiving rhythm gets lost in the daily relationships within a family or at school. Other, non-productive rhythms are set up that cause all kind of havoc in communicating. The possible kinds of non-rhythms include the following:

Giver	—	Giver
Giver	—	XXXX (Nobody's there)
Receiver	—	XXXX (Nobody's there)
Receiver	—	Receiver

Giver-Giver

The Giver-Giver non-rhythm occurs most frequently between parents and children. Inevitably this style leads to a game called Uproar, in which the two parties yell and scream at each other until one of them walks out and slams the door. Sometimes the door-banging happens physically and literally; most of the time it happens psychologically. Usually the child eventually shuts up, assumes a vacant distant gaze, looks away and folds his or her arms. The door has slammed. You sense that the child no longer hears a word you're saying. No communication has occurred; frustration and anger result.

Example: Mother is concerned about her fifteen year old's friends. They seem a rowdy bunch. She raises the subject to her daughter.

"Susan, I really don't like those kids you hang around with. Why can't you spend time with Kathy and Jill down the street?"

"Oh, Mom," she says with some irritation in her voice. "Why don't you get off my back about my friends? You're always complaining about them."

Mother responds with some irritation: "Well, those kids are out for no good. I've seen them in the park, drinking and smoking. You're much too young for such things."

"I'm fifteen years old. I'm no kid any longer," Susan shouts back. "Why do you treat me like a child?"

Mom's now more upset: "Now, you listen to me, young lady. I'm *telling* you I don't want you associating with those hoodlums anymore. Do you understand?"

"They are not hoodlums," Susan shouts back. "They're my friends and you can't stop me from being with them." At this point, Susan slams the door psychologically—and perhaps physically.

If mother goes on talking, it all falls on deaf ears. Susan will make no response at all. The rhythm of giving and receiving has never been established and the attempt at communication has only alienated mother and daughter.

As parents and educators we often teach our children this non-rhythm of communication by getting hooked into it so easily with the children. I encourage you to watch out for this Giver-Giver dynamic and to bail out when you get caught in it. You can bail out by refusing to communicate further until you both settle down. Or you can quit giving and become a receiver of the child's giving. This way you teach the child that Giving-Giving does not work.

Giver-No One's There

The second type of non-rhythm occurs when there is a Giver but there is no one there to receive. Usually the parent or teacher is the Giver and the child doesn't hear. The most common example takes place at meal time. It goes simply:

Mom: "Johnny, Susie, come and eat."

Johnny and Susie: No response. They continue watching Sesame Street.

Mom: "Johnny, Susie, turn off the TV and come and eat."

Johnny and Susie: No response.

Mom: (Voice raised) "Will you kids get in here this minute! How many times do I have to call?"

Johnny and Susie: No response.

This attempt at communication might go on for some time before the children respond. By then Mom's upset has reached the boiling point, the food has lost its boiling point, and the atmosphere around the table has grown tense and edgy. Mom attempted to be the Giver, but nobody received her message.

This rhythm takes another common form where the child wants to give, but the parent is not there. Children often seem to want to talk at apparently inconvenient times to adults—e.g., when Mom is preparing a meal or working on a project, when Dad is reading the paper or repairing the furnace. The child gives a message and the parent is too busy to receive it. This situation occurs more frequently than we might assume. We miss our children's messages when they casually toss them to us in a moment of our involvement in "something more important."

By stating this I do not want to suggest that we should always drop whatever we're doing when our children speak to us. That's asking a bit much. However, I would encourage you to attend more carefully to the times your children do address you. I believe that developing and maintaining an open and easy Giving and Receiving rhythm with your children is perhaps the most important thing you can do as a parent or teacher. Having your newspaper reading or your project interrupted by a child who wants to give you a message is of little consequence compared to the life-giving relationship you establish when you receive what he or she wants to give.

Receiver-No One To Give

The third non-rhythm finds a Receiver with no Giver. In this case, parents and teachers almost always take the position of Receiver with the child reluctant to give any message. How often have we wanted our children to tell us what happened and they respond with a nondescript, "Nothing"? "Where did you go?" gets a "Nowhere"; "what did you do?" receives a "Nothing"; and "whom were you with?" is honored with "No one special."

Even with very young children, we take the stance of Receiver, and they do not become Givers. At times, for reasons beyond our wisdom, very young children will simply not answer relatively simple questions. I might ask a three year old: "Jimmy, do you want to come to the store with me or stay home?" I sense that he really wants to come, but he stands there looking at me saying nothing. By asking the question I have placed myself in the position of receiving his yes or no. I want him to be the Giver. But he stands there. I get frustrated because the Giving-Receiving rhythm is broken. I want to know, to receive his position. He is not there as Giver for me. So upset might I become that I insist that he tell me now; I may even berate him and question his sanity—all due to the frustration that arises from the lack of a Giving-Receiving rhythm.

The more we insist that our children be Givers when we wish to be Receivers, the more likely our efforts will meet with resistance. None of us like being forced to reveal ourselves. Kids, especially, often perceive our questions as interrogation and sense that we are "checking up" on them. They don't like that "invasion" into their private space and so back away from us. (I will talk later about ways of approaching children so as not to alienate them.)

Receiver-Receiver

The fourth non-rhythm in communication happens more rarely than the others. When parent and child both stand as Receivers, they cause a breakdown in communication. In fact, two Receivers and no Givers equals silence in its pure form. Practically, this rhythm usually occurs during an argument and only briefly.

Let's say that a father and his son are arguing about the son's curfew time and they get into a rhythm of asking each other questions. It might go like this: After considerable arguing Father says: "What can you possibly do out till midnight anyway?"

Son responds: "What's so sacred about being in at 11:00 P.M.?"

Dad: "Don't other parents insist that their kids be home at a reasonable hour?"

Son: "How come you don't trust me to know how to take care of myself?"

At one level, these questions place each person in a position of Receiving. No communication is taking place. At a deeper level, all these questions are probably camouflaged statements making both father and son Givers. Either way no communication occurs.

Hopefully, you see now why the fundamental principle of communication is so vital—you must have, at all times, a *Giver* and a *Receiver* if you want to communicate. All other rhythms sabotage your efforts to reach your children and be reached in return.

An image that has helped me hold onto the idea of Giving and Receiving is that of two trapeze artists. Their act works only if one *gives* and the other *receives*. The woman usually swings out, lets go—gives—and is received by the man who has held on to his swing. Their act would be a bore if they both decided to receive the other—just swinging back and forth waiting for the other to give. More exciting, certainly, but more dangerous would be the case if they both decided to give at the same time. They would both swing out and let go of their swings at the same time, trying to reach each other in mid-air. Communication is much like the trapeze act. It works best when one gives and the other receives. The difference, of course, in a trapeze act is that the same persons usually do the giving and receiving. In communication the two artists both give and receive in a mutual rhythm.

Along with this most fundamental principle of giving and receiving, there is a critical rule of thumb or assumption helpful to make in teaching our children to communicate. Simply stated it says: *It is helpful to assume that I am the only one in the world who knows the principle of good communicating*—namely, there must always be a Giver and a Receiver. I assume this because I then take responsibility for making communication happen.

This is especially true when two people are wanting to give messages at the same time. If I want real communication to take place, then I need to defer giving my message and receive the other's message before that person will be able to receive me. Certainly, in dealing with children I cannot expect them to defer giving when we are both in giving stances. An illustration of two people giving gifts clarifies this point.

It's Christmas time and John knows Jill just loves bean bag chairs. Jill knows that John also thinks bean bag chairs are the most comfortable of all chairs. So they buy one for each other. They come together to give their presents, and John says, "Here Jill, this is for you. Take it."

Now, her arms are full of her present to him, so she cannot receive his. And she insists: "No, John, I want to give this present to you. Please take it."

But he cannot take it since he is holding her present. You see, when both parties stand as Givers, everyone ends up frustrated. Somebody has to defer and say: "Wait a second; we are both interested in giving each other our gifts. Let me set down my gift to you, and then I can have free hands to receive your gift to me. Then, after I've received your gift, your hands will be empty and you will be able to receive my gift."

Chapter 4

Receiving:
The Skill of Listening

To develop a Giving-Receiving rhythm in conversation we begin with Receiving. Listening is the more difficult part of communication and the most frequently violated aspect in parent-child, teacher-child relations. It may even be the more vital dimension of a Giving-Receiving rhythm.

The word "communication" suggests as much. Made up of three roots it tells us that to communicate means *standing with another's unique perception of the world.* The first part of the word, COMM, comes from the Latin preposition "cum" meaning *with.* UNIC is derived from an Anglo-Saxon word meaning "unique." And ATION is a Latin suffix denoting *action* in English. Thus, communication is a very *active* process whereby a person stands *with* the *uniqueness* of another.

COMM	UNIC	ATION
stands with	uniqueness	active process

So, when you actively stand with another's experience you are in communication. You are attending to, recognizing, and affirming the person. To do that effectively, you want to be a good receiver. The best way children will learn to stand empathically with another is through their experience of us standing with them. We teach communication by our ability to communicate ourselves.

Stay Away from Self

Receiving messages involves two simple but quite difficult steps. First, you try as hard as possible to stay away from your own experience, and stand with your child's perception. You try to let the child lead you through the various paths of his or her perception. Most of us have a natural tendency to relate what others tell us to our own past histories. For example, Jim says: "I sure hate going to the dentist." And Sue replies: "Oh, yeah, I get nervous just thinking about it."

Jim and Sue both remain locked in their own worlds. Fortunately, in this example, the Giver is making small talk and does not seem heavily invested in his message. But what happens when a child believes that his message is important and the parent remains in his or her own world and does not enter the child's experience? The dialogue might go like this:

Sam, fifteen years old: (in a complaining voice) "School's really awful. All the teachers are loading us down with work. We don't even have time to enjoy stuff."

Dad: "You think you have it bad. When I went to high school we used to have at least two hours of homework every night. I never see you bring a book home at all."

In this case, the son has not been received. Dad stayed in his own world and failed to enter his son's experience. We have two Givers and no real communication.

To let go of your experience and enter your child's takes a lot of practice. The next time you talk with another person, try to observe how frequently you let what he or she says bounce off your experience, and then, in response, you share your own experience. Usually, when others are trying to give you an important message, they do not want to know about, nor do they care, if the same thing happened to you years ago. They need to have their message received, not used as an invitation to you to share your life's experience.

The classic example is the child who wants his dad to drive him to school this morning because it's twenty-five degrees outside. And dad says: "Listen, young man, when I was your age I used to walk three miles to school everyday in the snow without boots because we were so poor." Dad has remained in his own world. The child experiences non-understanding and senses that his world does not count for his father.

Another factor makes it more difficult for you as parents to receive the messages of your children—you are emotionally involved in their lives. As parents you nurture your children, attending to their physical and psychological safety. This dynamic leads you to respond with extreme quickness to many messages they give. The quick responses come from your nurturing desire to immediately take away any pain they experience.

Your three year old falls down and scrapes her leg and you quickly pick her up and say: "Oh, there, there, everything will be OK"; or "Ssh, ssh, don't cry. It's nothing big, just a little scrape." You see, the effort is to solve the difficulty without *first* receiving the message from the child's point of view, namely, that "I fell down and hurt my knee, and I need some attention from you."

If a parent or teacher simply tried to receive the child's message, instead of "making it better," he or she would say instead: "Oh, Suzy, I see you fell down and scraped your leg. Sometimes coming to Mom and getting a hug makes you fell better, right?" This way the child has experienced the giving-receiving rhythm of communication: she has sensed her mother standing with her in her unique perception of the world, and her physical hurt has naturally drifted away without any suggestion that crying is bad.

The same applies to older children who lose a game or don't make the team. Our parental tendency quickly focuses on lifting the child's sadness. Can you slow down that fast response? Rather than jump in too soon with your healing ointments, can you, instead, simply receive your child's disappointment? The nurturer in you might spontaneously want to say: "Oh, that's OK. You'll make the team next year, I'm sure."

But the Receiver in you might respond: "I know how disappointed you must be. You really worked hard to make the team."

The most nurturing ointment you can administer is to stand with your child's unique experience of disappointment. If he knows you understand and have received his message he will heal himself. Furthermore, you also teach him by your modeling how to receive others without saving them.

Slowing down your desire to give when your children have given is the key to becoming a good Receiver. Because we work to protect our children we oftentimes answer their statements with authoritative statements of our own *before* we have received their full message. If you want your children to slow down and listen, then you must slow down and listen when they talk.

For example, while sitting at the dinner table a teenage boy states: "I can't understand why smoking pot is illegal. There isn't anything wrong with it."

And Dad answers quickly: "I'll tell you one thing. If I ever catch you smoking that stuff, all hell will break loose."

The father brings to the boy's message an authoritative proclamation based on *his own* perception of what is good for the boy. The difficulty here is that son and father cannot communicate when both stand as Givers. The father would greatly facilitate the giving-receiving rhythm if he could stand back from his nurturing and authoritative position and *first* receive the message of his son. So the initial step is: Stay away from your own experience, and only attend to the world of the Giver.

Tell Back What You Have Received

The second step in being a good Receiver is to tell the Giver what you have received. If you cannot do that you have not fully understood the message.

In the classroom, teachers (Givers) structure the communication process with the students (Receivers) by giving them tests. The implication is: "I have given you a message. Now if you can tell it back to me in your own words, then I'll know that you understand me."

In most family communications we don't have tests, but the Giver, just like the teacher, needs to know if the other party really got the message. The only way he or she will know that is if the Receiver can give back the main sense of what was communicated.

An example helps: A thirteen year old girl comes home from school and in an irritated voice says: "Teachers are all jerks. They're so unfair it's unreal. They're always picking the same drippy kids for everything." When Mom is following the two steps for receiving—getting away from her own experience and attending to the Giver, and telling back what she received—then Mom will say: "So you're pretty upset with some teachers because they seem to favor some kids over others." When daughter says, "Yeah, I sure am upset. The stupid idiot," then Mom knows she has received well. A receiving mother will go right on receiving.

Mom: "In fact, just thinking about those teachers really bugs you."

Daughter: "It sure does. You know, it would feel nice once in a while to be noticed. I mean, I do go to school there."

Mom: "Sometimes you feel as though you're just part of the woodwork and no one really cares if you're there or not."

Daughter: "Well, they don't care. If they did they would have said something to me about that little article I wrote in the school paper."

Mom: "It still sort of hurts your feelings that the teachers didn't compliment you on that article."

Daughter: "Well, I suppose it wasn't very good but I worked like crazy on it and was so excited when they said they'd print it."

Mom: "At times you think it might not have been a good article because no one said much, even though after you wrote it you thought it was pretty good."

Daughter: "Well, it was pretty good, I think."

You'll notice that the mother gives no messages; she is the Receiver. She gives no advice, no solutions, no suggestions and no proclamations. She only receives. And she knows she's on target when her daughter affirms her receiving responses with a "Yes" or "That's exactly right" and then goes on.

In receiving and telling back what you have heard, it is helpful to attend to the *content* of the message and to the *feeling* tone of the Giver. The deeper level of receiving picks up the feeling the Giver sends. Often this is left unsaid verbally. However, it gets communicated through tone of voice, body language, facial expression and vocal sounds (e.g., sighing, grunting, crying, etc.). If you can give back the feeling you receive along with the content of the message, the Giver will really experience you "standing with his or her uniqueness."

A child's best friend moves away, and although the girl says nothing she mopes around the house looking sad. She is a Giver sending a strong message. A Receiving parent could say to her: "Jill, you seem pretty sad ever since Mary left." Jill might say "Yeah" and begin talking about it, or she might nonchalantly shrug it off and say "Nah, I'm OK." In either case, if the parent received the feeling accurately, that daughter experienced the parent as "standing with her uniqueness." Just standing with Jill's loss already helps her to heal the hurt. She senses that she is not alone. The issue may not need to be pursued any further.

Rules in Teaching Children To Listen Well

1. Let go of your own experience as best as you can and enter the Giver's world.

2. Tell back the feeling and the content you have received from the Giver.

Chapter 5

Giving:
The Skill of Sending
Direct Messages

Parents and teachers often ask me what they can do when their children refuse to talk or be the Giver. Perhaps the most effective method in teaching children to share in a self-revealing way is for the parent or teacher to become an even more attentive Receiver. The evident statement children make by their silence is just that—they choose to remain silent. So you try receiving that and say: "You seem very quiet tonight, John." He grunts, but he has experienced you noticing and attending to him.

At this point you might try to note the feeling tone he presents. Does he seem discouraged, angry, simply reflective, antagonistic, happy? I believe that parents and teachers should trust their instincts here. Children's feelings are communicated to us partially through our own feelings. So if you sense a particular feeling emanating from your child, chances are you are correct.

Let's say you sense antagonism from your child John, but he says nothing. You might receive that message by saying: "John I get the feeling you're quite angry with someone." Silence. "Am I right?"

If he says "Yeah," you can ask with whom, or you might just stay receiving: "So, when you're feeling that angry with someone you tend to get pretty quiet."

He might go with that. If he doesn't, and remains silent, you then respect his choice not to share with you at that time. But you want to realize that your brief receiving has been experienced by him as a positive moment. You have noticed and stood with his uniqueness. And, in doing so, you have laid one more small brick in the edifice of his positive self-esteem. He has experienced someone special accepting him just as he is.

Perhaps the central reason young people choose not to talk with their parents is that they don't really believe that the parents will receive them anyway. One of the most frustrating dynamics I encounter as a family therapist is the teenager who refuses to talk with the parents anymore because he or she believes that the parents "will not understand me and can't change anyway." If children believe that their messages will not be received by parents, they eventually learn not to give.

Parents often set their kids up. They ask them a question such as: "Jan, whom did you go with to the party?" Jan becomes the Giver and tells. Then, instead of receiving the message, Mom jumps on her statement and gives a message in return: "I sure wish you would find some different friends." You see, if Jan's messages are not simply received, and she gets negative messages in return, she will learn to remain silent when Mom wants her to be a Giver. Only when Mom truly wants to stand in Jan's world and receive her world will Jan open up to Mom. If Jan senses that Mom will disapprove or give a long lecture in return, Jan will learn quickly that not talking is the smart and safe road to travel with Mom.

"But," you say, "I can't agree with everything my kids say." No, you can't. You have your world of values and beliefs also. *But understanding and agreeing are not the same.* When you understand your child you simply stand in his or her world and see it from that viewpoint. You suspend judgment, which means not comparing your child's view against your view. Only *after* you have fully understood the other view—stood with your child— then you can return to your own world and compare his or her view against yours. If your views differ, you are then free to say so.

For example, eight year old Beth decides she hates broccoli and states her position clearly. You first want to stand with her perception of broccoli—it feels funny in the mouth and tastes like bushes. After that, you may return to your own world and the value you place on Beth eating a well-balanced dinner. Now, you can disagree with her decision not to eat. The entire process takes ten seconds. You say: "Beth, I know you don't like broccoli because of the odd way it feels and tastes (that's understanding), but I want you to eat it because it's good for you." First, you try to understand; then, only after you have stood in Beth's world, do you agree or disagree if necessary.

This style of receiving your children best begins in their infancy. Before they begin talking you can begin receiving the many messages they give through tears, grunts, and smiles. If you stand in their world momentarily and let them know what message you have received from them, as they grow up they will naturally learn how to communicate with you. And, more importantly, they will experience their world as valued and worthy of notice. And that is how self-esteem is developed.

Furthermore, as you practice receiving your young children, you will learn excellent communication habits and will grow in respect for your children's worlds. It takes diligent effort and great attention to the small cues your children give. For instance, when Ann cries as you set her in a tub of water, you might say: "I know you don't like this much, Ann." When Dave smiles as you enter the room, you will respond: "Oh, I see you're happy that I'm here to get you."

A word of caution if you are beginning this process now with teenagers. They will notice that you are doing something different and might object. They might say: "Why are you repeating everything I'm saying?" or "What book have you been reading now?" Don't stop. Stay with it. The children are resisting any changes in the usual patterns around the house.

If children experience you listening to them, respecting their input without judging it quickly, they will more easily become the Giver in the communication rhythm. If the atmosphere between you and the children is full of trust and interest, then the groundwork is laid for them to become more verbally expressive of all that moves within.

Once you have laid this receiving and respectful foundation on which your children can give messages, what principles of Giving do you want to teach?

First of all, you want the children to own their own concerns and problems and not project them onto others. You can best understand this principle by seeing it in your own communicating patterns. And you can best teach this principle to children by practicing it yourself in conversing with them.

Let's say Johnny is chewing gum with his mouth open and popping it with his teeth while you are reading a book. You become annoyed. Who has the problem, your son or you? Clearly you do. Johnny has no problem with his own behavior. You are the one troubled by his gum chewing. Thus, when you give a message to your son about the chewing noise, you want him to know *you* have the problem, not him. So you say: "Johnny, *I* get annoyed when you chew so loudly and it distracts me from my reading." If you believed the problem was his you would say: "What's the matter with *you*, making all that noise!"

When Susy brings home a poor report card and you get upset, who has the problem? You do. You are the one worried about her future. Certainly, she may eventually have a problem if she doesn't get passing grades, but at the present moment that doesn't bother her. You are the one upset. Thus, you have the problem.

Consequently, when you speak to your child you want to share *your* problem with her behavior. If you lay the problem on her shoulders you do two things:

1) You act in a dishonest way, not stating reality as it is.
2) You teach her that her behavior makes her an inadequate or bad person.

This second effect stands as the potentially most damaging. When parents blame children for their own difficulties, they often do so with phrases such as:

"What's the matter with you?" (by which the parent means: "Something is the matter with you.")

"How dumb can you get?"

"Can't you see what you're doing?"

"I've seen stupid things in my day, but what you just did takes the cake!"

"You apologize this instant (implied is the concluding phrase) you bad boy!"

"You must have water on your brain!"

These kinds of statements are experienced as attacks on the child. The *child* is declared dumb or inadequate in a situation where the parent or teacher has the problem.

Once you own the problem, you now have particular strategies to employ in communicating with your child. The first is to make a *simple request.* If your daughter's stereo is blaring from top to bottom of the house, and you have a problem with this, you first make a simple request: "Susy, will you please turn down your stereo?"

If a simple request does not work, then you want to present Susy with a full and direct message about *your problem.* You want her to know how you are feeling about her behavior and how it is directly affecting your life. So you might say: "Susy, I get annoyed when you play your music so loudly that I'm distracted from reading this book." In this message Susy knows that the problem is in you (you are annoyed) and she knows the effect of her specific behavior on you (you are distracted and cannot concentrate). Nothing in your statement suggests anything wrong with her as a fifteen year old girl in love with loud music.

Will she respond and turn down the volume? I believe that she is more likely to attend to your need for "undistractable noise" if you don't back her into a corner with a strong statement about *her.* If you command and demand her to "turn it down," you may get immediate, although uncooperative results. But you run the risk of setting up a barrier between Susy and yourself, a barrier of resistance.

Generally, in interpersonal relations, if one person exerts force over the other, that second person will attempt to resist the force. Susy may resist a command by turning the stereo down only one notch. Then you must holler up again, at which point she proclaims that she did turn the music down and that if she turns it down any further she won't be able to hear it.

Perhaps the most important advantage to sending full and direct messages has to do with modeling openness to your child. If you share your feelings with Susan and the effect of her behavior on you, you are telling her about yourself and showing her how one reveals self in communication.

At times most of us become frustrated when we want our children to be self-revealing and they resist; yet how many of us are self-revealing to them? I believe that it is very helpful for us to share with our children our own deep thoughts and feelings, especially if we hope that our children will disclose themselves to us.

Another advantage of sharing yourself with Susan is that you are appealing to her basic humanness to respond to your needs. In many ways children display considerable self-centeredness. They may not often show empathy toward parents or other family members. One way for them to learn other-centeredness and sensitivity to family members lies in your efforts to present your own needs before the children. If you start by demanding that Susan turn down the stereo, she will not respond to you as a person with needs, but solely as a powerful authority. Such a strong presentation does not allow the child the opportunity to attend to your needs as a person; instead it drives her more deeply into herself.

Let's carry on this dialogue further. Suppose Susie responds to your direct statement by saying: "Oh, Dad, it's not that noisy. Just practice shutting it out of your mind."

Now, you need to switch gears and *receive* her message. Then you *give* her your message again. You say: "Susie, I know you'd like me to block the music out (Receiving), but I'm trying to say to you that with the music so loud I am finding it very difficult to concentrate. Would you please turn it down so I can read this book?" (Giving)

Hopefully, Susie will attend to your need. If she does not, then you have a new problem, namely expressing your need, inviting her to respond to it person to person, and her choosing not to do so. You now deal with your new problem by saying:

"Susy, I feel badly that you don't seem to care about the effect your music has on me. I had really hoped you could see my difficulty and help me out by turning down the volume."

You see how you appeal to Susie's human sensitivity and how you continue to deal with whatever problem you are experiencing at the moment—first, the irritation over the volume of the stereo; second, the hurt arising from her reluctance to respond to your need. Of course, if she still doesn't respond, then you might have to take a different approach (to be discussed in Chapter 7). If a child consistently fails to respond to the expression of a parent's needs, some other dynamics are probably operative, such as a power conflict between parent and child or strong hostility between the two in which the child is "out to get" the parent at every turn.

Here are some other situations where a direct message would be the appropriate response when you are having a problem with your child's behavior.

Four year old Tony continues listening to Sesame Street after you have called him to dinner three times. You might say: "Tony, I'm getting a little irritated with your watching Sesame Street after you've been called three times to eat. Our food is getting cold while we're waiting for you and it doesn't taste as good to me so cold."

Eight year old Betty pokes along whenever you want to go someplace. You say: "I'm getting quite impatient, Betty, with you taking so long to get ready because we will be late for the program."

Twelve year old Tom cuts the grass faithfully, but often doesn't do the trimming which is part of the job. You give: "Tom, I'm really pleased with your cutting the grass every week. It's quite a big help to me; but I get displeased when I see the trimming not done and I have to look at an untidy yard."

Sixteen year old Tina fails to keep curfew time by forty-five minutes. You say when she walks in: "Tina, I was very worried when you didn't come home on time and couldn't get to sleep. Now I'm angry because you didn't call and let me know what was happening."

Talking to your children with full messages also makes it more difficult for them to interpret what you say inaccurately. When you give messages in indirect or incomplete ways, you present your children with a blank-filled statement. Remember when as a child in school you had work sheets for English with sentences in which you were supposed to fill in the missing blanks.

> Johnny _____ the ball and _____ it to
> the _____.

As the author of that sentence I know what words go in the blanks. But you do not. Yet most likely you will put some words in, and hope you guessed correctly. Try it. Fill in the missing blanks in the sentence above. You received my communication accurately if you guessed:

Johnny *kicked* the ball and *rolled* it to the *goalie.*

If you enjoy soccer you might have gotten the "right answer" more easily than if you were a baseball player. Usually when we fill in missing blanks in another's communication, we do so out of *our* experience rather than theirs. Our children do the same thing. If, for example, a child has a low self-image and the parent says "What's the matter with you breaking that bowl? How clumsy can you get?" the child will fill in all the missing blanks in a negative way. He will likely conclude that something *is* the matter with him—with the whole him, that he is clumsy in *everything* he touches, and that his dad not only doesn't like what he did, but now no longer likes the child. Dad may not have meant any of those things, but that's what the child "got."

Instead, a full message would have protected against some misinterpretation. "I get very irritated when you break a dish because it costs money and I have to go to the store and get a new one." This statement makes it much more difficult for the child to "fill in the missing blanks."

Sending messages directly and fully also helps us avoid preaching and lecturing our children. Most youngsters (as well as adults) find a lecturing person difficult to listen to; they tend to resist such people.

One family I worked with had a father who lectured, preached and philosophized most Saturday mornings. As a captive audience the entire family sat absorbing the barrage of words that came from the father's mouth. Within themselves they resisted whatever he said. They told me: "Now, whenever he opens his mouth we just tune out." To help the father we worked on sending direct and full messages, and tried to teach him to cut down on the volume of words he used. To accomplish this, I had the family buy egg timers, set them in strategic areas of the house. Whenever someone started lecturing, the other person could turn over the timer and when the salt ran out three minutes later the lecturer had to quit speaking. Young people know that most things can be said in less than three minutes. Parents and teachers know it too, I think, but we aren't convinced that the kids got the message, so we tend to go on and on until they get it.

Teaching children to be self-revealing Givers can best be accomplished by our own self-revelations. We want them to learn to own their own concerns and problems and not project them onto others. We also want them to speak in as full and direct a manner as possible. By giving to them our full statements and attentively listening to theirs, we help to create for them the wonderful experience of human bonding.

Rules in Teaching Children To Talk Well

1. As parent or teacher, create a receptive atmosphere by listening attentively.

2. Try to be as self-revealing to the children as you wish them to be with you.

3. Teach them to own their own concerns and problems.

4. Teach them to express themselves in a full and direct manner.

Chapter 6

Teaching Children to Believe and Think Realistically

Many beliefs children learn when they are young form and influence the rest of their lives. I remember vividly a friend of our family taking my brother, age eight, and me, age six, to an amusement park in Chicago, and "strongly encouraging" us to ride the ominous roller coaster. We were terrified. To this day I have not been on a roller coaster. Open air heights bother me — my feet tingle, my imagination sees me hurtling to the ground, and I stand three feet back from the rail.

Now, my children are learning to fear heights too, I'm afraid. I caution them about getting too close to the edge; I reach out to hold their hands and say more often than is helpful, "Be careful." (My wife also may have picked up my beliefs about heights. She once parachuted out of an airplane, but now acts as "neurotic" as I do about being up high.)

Generally, beliefs about heights do not interface with productive living. However, other beliefs developed in childhood may radically influence the very basis of our personality. Last night a twenty-five year old woman came to me in a chronically depressed state. She wasn't sure why she felt down. She reported acting in a superior way toward other people, which seemed to turn them off. She ended up without close friends.

As we talked it became evident what triggered the superiority reaction. She had developed a belief early in life that she was less valued than her three sisters. In order to gain equality with them in her parents' eyes, she began acting in a superior way. Because she now continues to believe she is "less than" others, she still responds by acting superior as a way of compensating for the belief of inferiority.

Children's beliefs and thoughts create their feelings and behaviors. The critical element determining a child's "personality style" lies in the beliefs that he or she has about self, others and the world. If Tony believes, for instance, that the world around him is a friendly and relatively safe place, his way of navigating in it will be free and loose; if he believes it to be a threatening and dangerous world, he will react in a cautious, perhaps rigid manner. The reaction is based on his *beliefs*.

Oftentimes I hear parents say about their children: "Well, that's just the way she is," or "He was cut out of a different fabric than she." Well, the differences in children's personalities can be discovered in the varied beliefs they have picked up. Their beliefs determine how they act and feel. I cannot emphasize this point too much. If you recognize that your children's personality development is based on what they come to believe, then you know that their thinking apparatus is what demands your full attention. The key to helping your children function in a fully human way throughout life lies in your responsiveness to their thoughts and beliefs. Your job is to assist them in thinking in a realistic, sensible and accurate manner about themselves, others, and their world.

Realistic believing generally leads to sound mental functioning. When your children's beliefs become unrealistic and irrational, then trouble lies ahead. The difficulty, of course, rests in the fact that children (and adults) are convinced that what they believe is realistic and rational. Otherwise they would quit believing it. But just because kids or parents believe something does not make it true. If your daughter believes you are old-fashioned, her belief does not make you so. If your son believes the discipline he received at school is unfair, it does not make it so.

Practically, we want to pay close attention to the beliefs our children present. Those that are reasonable and realistic we want to reinforce; those that are not based on reality and are irrational we want to challenge.

Let's look at some of the unrealistic and irrational beliefs of our children. These are the kinds of beliefs that can sabotage our children's happiness now and as they grow into adulthood.

1. Drama and Catastrophe

Children think bigger than life oftentimes. They do that, in part, because they are so little and the world looks so big. They also learn dramatic thinking from us as parents. We reinforced their learning experiences by our dramatic responses. Jill eats her noodles with a fork for the first time, and we react by clapping and saying in an excited voice: "Oh, Jill, how wonderful. Look, everyone, how Jill is eating with a fork. Oh boy!" By no means am I suggesting that we should not teach our children by using drama. Kids learn that way. However, a negative spin-off does occur—they learn to think in dramatic ways.

Children also learn dramatic thought from our dramatic responses. In order to make a point we will magnify it to our children with a broad generalization or all-inclusive remark. We say things like: "Don't you *ever* do that again"; "You *never* come home on time"; "You *always* sass back"; "Keep that up and I will drop you out of the car right here, and you can walk home"; "I cannot believe anyone could be so dumb as to pull a stunt like that."

Another source of children's dramatic thought process lies in nursery rhymes. Many of these rhymes present catastrophic situations. Humpty Dumpty cannot be put back together again (isn't that awful); Jack and Jill came tumbling down and Jack broke his crown—he broke his head. There were three *blind* mice, who got their tails cut off with a carving knife; London Bridge came falling down, and so on. We put the children to bed and sing, "When the bough breaks the cradle will fall, and down will come baby, cradle and all. Good night!" Then we turn off the lights and say, "Sleep tight; don't let the bedbugs bite." And our little children imagine giant black bugs gnawing away at their flesh. Or the children learn to pray: "If I should die before I wake,

I pray the Lord my soul to take." Now, these are catastrophic kinds of thoughts.

With this kind of dramatic thinking, we can easily see why our children upset themselves. In their minds they make events bigger than life. Thus, they carry burdens much too heavy for one young person to bear.

A fifteen year old girl was brought into counseling by her mother because of a suicide attempt. She was having a slight acne problem and thought dramatically: "I am so ugly; no one will ever like me again." Because she truly believed this, you can understand why she might want to end it all.

Not long ago, I listened to a ten year old girl tell her mother, recently divorced and struggling financially, "Mother, you *never* do anything for me. You *never* give me any money to do stuff. But you *always* go and buy clothes and shoes and things for yourself. You are so *selfish*. You *only* think of yourself and *never* think of me." In fact, the child receives a dollar-a-week allowance. This drama strengthened the child's belief that she is alone in the world, abandoned not only by her father at the time of the divorce, but now also by a mother who "never pays attention" (and money) to her.

Practically, you can do some things to help your children moderate their catastrophic thinking. First of all, your own ability to think reasonably and realistically will serve as a model to your children. Pay attention to the way you talk with your youngsters. Watch out for words and phrases that make things bigger than life, such as, "always, never, absolutely, it is awful, I'm totally shocked, I can't stand it any longer, this is simply incredible, I am devastated," and so on. Moderate the strength of these phrases to "often, this a difficult situation, quite a surprise, I'm feeling the strain," etc.

Secondly, don't let yourself get hooked into your children's drama. Often you might "swallow" their beliefs, and then get caught in believing their unreal world. Certainly you want to stand with their experience of the world. You want to understand that's how they are experiencing it at the moment, but you do not want to identify with it to such a degree that you end up feeling as anxious or saddened as they are.

Say your sixteen year old daughter Ann comes home "crushed" (now there's a catastrophic word if I've ever heard one) because she did not get elected to the student council. She's aimed toward and worked for this position for a number of weeks. Her disappointment "knows no bounds." Of course, as the parent, you feel sad for her. You want to stand with her feelings, *but* you do not want to take on her sadness and her dramatic beliefs that keep the sadness alive. You want to understand that *she* feels sad and thinks: "This just crushes me." But you also want to hold onto your own, more realistic, position that "in the great scheme of life's events, this is a temporary disappointment of relatively mild proportions."

Certainly, you do not tell her that at the moment of her crisis, when her feelings are so strong. But you will help her by realizing within herself the actual seriousness of the situation. By avoiding "being hooked" by her feelings, you maintain your own solid position in the real world and you offer her a firm grabbing-on place. In your stability and moderate reaction to this "most serious crisis," Ann can learn that life goes on amid the joys and disappointments of daily existence. She also learns that to have people standing with each other in times of difficulty far exceeds the value of attaining successes and achievements in life.

A third thing you can do to help your children dedramatize their thoughts is to talk with them in a non-catastrophic and calm way *after* the emotions have subsided. After Ann has released her disappointment, then you might say: "Ann, I sensed how badly you felt about losing that election, and I saw how much it meant to you. Now that it's over I'm also hopeful that you can see that getting into that election race is a sign of an alive, active person. And that's a neat thing about you. The only way you will succeed in things is by doing what you did—jumping in with both feet. When you jump in life, sometimes you will win and sometimes you will lose. Although it's tough to lose at times, I really like the fact that you keep on jumping in. That's the attitude of a winner."

2. "Must" Beliefs

Children learn very early in life to become little legislators, making up rules for the way life "should be." They dictate how parents *ought* to respond, how brothers and sisters *must* play with them, how teachers *have to* behave, and how the home *should be* run. Their wishes and desires become internal demands.

When children insist that the world be other than the way it is, they learn how to become angry and intolerant. Life flows much more peacefully if children can accept differences among people. Racism, sexism, agism, all the forms of prejudice are based on beliefs about the way people and things should be. If they are not the way they should be, they are bad or inadequate.

Children also can place demands on themselves, thus making it very difficult for them to be self-tolerant. "I have to get straight A's; I must have a date for the prom; I absolutely need the car," etc. If they don't reach their own goals, then they feel defeated and "no good." They often find it hard to tolerate limitedness in themselves because they "should be able to do it." They then become angry with themselves and don't like who they are.

While hopes and desires and goals can serve children well, demanding within themselves that these goals must be attained, even after they have not been reached, can be very defeating and frustrating to children. To reach for the stars is fine, but when their efforts fall short, their ability to accept their own limitedness will help them gracefully "go back to the drawing board" and try again, rather than give up in discouragement and self-disdain. (More will be discussed on the "tyranny of the shoulds" in chapter 14.)

What can you do as parents and teachers to help your children be more tolerant and accepting of the way things are rather than the way they *must* be?

First, you can learn to accept more graciously your children's differences with you. The more you can accept their world and reactions as those of most normal children, the less "shoulding" you will do as parents. Tolerating differences between you and your children models for them a way of peaceful living in a highly pluralistic society. Tolerating those differences does not mean you have to agree with the children; it only means accepting the fact that the differences exist, and both positions are valid simply because they are there.

Second, when your children place heavy demands on how others must be, you, at times, can talk with them directly about how people are different, and how they think and react out of their beliefs about what is best. This kind of teaching discussion can work if it's not done too frequently.

3. Fairness

One of the most popular internal demands that children make is that the world should be "fair." I have noticed that the actual notion of fairness as used by children and adults is an extremely relative term. Practically, I think "fairness" is defined as "the process whereby I got my way." Unfairness is defined as "the process whereby I didn't get my way."

If Toni makes the cheerleaders, then she declares, "That was really a fair way of picking kids." If she doesn't get selected, then, "That was really unfair; they didn't give some of us enough chance to practice before the trials." As adults we do much the same thing. Usually we too label as "fair" that process whereby a favorable outcome was attained by us.

Children can hook us quite easily into the game of "Fair vs. Unfair." When they bring up the claim of unfair, that is their bait to catch us in an argument whereby they hope to get their way. The label "unfair" is one that most of us parents don't like, because we believe we are being fair. In fact, we go out of our way to be fair. So we defend ourselves. Of course, we end up in an argument. The children are upset because they didn't get their way; we, as parents or teachers, are upset because our children do not seem grateful for all the ways we try to be generous with them.

You see, the issue of "fairness" is really not the concern at all. It is the diversionary tactic to cloud the real issue; it is also a way for children to use leverage against their parents to induce guilt in them. The real issue is that the children did not get what they wanted and they think they *should* (the internal demands) get it, or that they are entitled to get the same treatment as their brothers or sisters.

I think the most effective way to handle this approach from your children is to avoid the temptation to get into a debate on "fairness." Stick with the message underneath. And that message is: "I'm upset because I did not get what I wanted."

Michael, age nine, has to go to bed at 9:00 P.M. on school nights. His brother, Peter, age eleven, must go to bed at 9:30 P.M. Michael complains about how unfair that is. Instead of debating him on how Peter is older and when he, Michael, is eleven he will be able to stay up until 9:30, get right to the heart of the matter. Receive his real message under the words, by saying something like: "Mike, I realize that you don't like going to bed at 9:00 P.M. and wish you could stay up later." When he continues to complain and labels you unfair, say: "I can see you're upset because this didn't work out to your advantage. I'm sorry for you that it didn't, but the rules will still stay the same."

By moving away from discussions of fairness with your children, you gradually teach them that the world is not always a "fair" place in the true sense of the word. The world is a real place where injustice and inequality take place, where some people have more and some less, where what is called "fair" by one might be called "unfair" by another, and where most of the time people believe they are acting in a fair way. In other words, by getting under the labels "fair" and "unfair," you aid your children in dealing with the real issues of their life. As they get away from labeling situations "unfair" when they or others do not gain what they wanted, they will begin to realize that life is simply the way it is. They will learn to take off the heavy "shoulds" about the way it must be, and instead, more tolerantly, accept the flawed and limited world as it is.

Once they accept that things and people simply are the way they are, then they can work more diligently to change things to a greater justice for all. So, I am not saying to teach your children indifference about injustice. I am saying, however, that the label "unfair" serves as a smoke screen whereby children and adults do not accept the reality of the world as it is, and instead continue to upset themselves by demanding within themselves that "all must be fair." The fact is that all is not fair. Once they accept that, and let go of the demand that it "has to be fair," then they are freed to calmly and reasonably attempt to correct any injustices that might exist.

4. Blame and Name-Calling

With relative ease children can enter into a way of thinking that leads to name-calling and blame. The irrationality of such a style lies in the jump from a specific piece of behavior to a statement about the whole person. Willie leaps from an act by his teacher correcting him to a statement about what a "creep" she is. Mary hears her mother say, "You must be home by 11:00 P.M.," and she jumps to a statement about the whole parent: "You're so old-fashioned."

The leap from the single event to a universal statement about a person will obviously begin coloring a child's view of the other person. If a child begins doing the same thing with himself or herself, that child will soon view the self according to the name he or she calls him or herself. If Billy always calls himself a jerk when he makes a mistake, he soon will view himself as a jerk, unable to do much of anything.

Labeling self or others, especially with derogatory names, cuts into the respect a child can develop toward self or others. If Mary believes that Dad and Mom are "old-fashioned," that label will highly affect Mary's attentiveness to any messages from the parents. If she sees her teacher as a "weirdo," her ability to respect what the teacher says will be eroded. If she thinks of boys as dummies, black people as lazy, adults as old-fashioned, teachers as prudes, and police as pigs, you can readily see how she will lose respect for these individuals. If she sees herself as ugly, inferior, a little twerp, etc., she will certainly lose respect for herself. Thus, name-calling sabotages children's respect for others and for themselves.

As parents or teachers, you do not have total control over protecting your children from name-calling thoughts. They hear labels thrown about all around them. Little friends call each other "sissy" or "tattle-tale." Older children hear a wide variety of labels given to each other, many of which cannot be reprinted here.

You can, however, watch your own name-calling as parents and educators. Hopefully, you are already sensitive to not labeling your children based on their behavior. But you might also check your name-calling of other people as well. I have caught myself calling people "jerks" because of the way they drive, or "idiots" because of their political beliefs. Somehow my manner of disagreement with a behavior or a viewpoint ended in a derogatory statement about a person. When my children experience that jump from me, it does not take much to imitate.

The spirit underneath that I want to convey is that of deep reverence and respect for human beings. If I truly believe that the world is made up of a wide variety of human beings, all of whom have a right to function in a way that is life-giving, then I will focus only on behavior and beliefs, not on persons, when I disagree. If I can realize "there is a reason for that kind of behavior from that person" I will refrain from labeling the whole person, and only deal with the behavior or belief before me.

Eliminate labels and name-calling, and you are on your way to teaching your children respect for others and themselves, and you will aid them in avoiding a giant thinking trap—jumping from individual events to broad judgments about other people and about their own selves.

5. Good and Bad, Right and Wrong Beliefs

After being a psychotherapist for a number of years, I gradually began realizing that the words "good, bad, right, and wrong" were leaving my active vocabulary. I noticed that I internally cringed when others would say those words, whether in therapy or out. At home, I noticed, too, that every time one of my children uttered one of "those words," I jumped in and attempted to replace it with words like "helpful or unhelpful, workable or unworkable."

I wondered if I was losing my sense of moral rectitude. Were all moral values leaving me? I did not think so, because I still believed very much in ways of acting for the growth of people, and away from their harm or destruction in any way. So I thought I still had a strong moral sense, but was thinking of it in terms other than good or bad. The terms I was thinking in had to do with "what is helpful to human growth and what is harmful to human growth."

I was moving away from "good, bad, right and wrong" because I was seeing so many adults filled with negative beliefs of self, intolerance of others, blame toward others and guilt toward self. When I heard them talk, their language was chock full of those good-bad words.

"Bad" and "wrong," of course, cause more difficulty than the positive labels. These judgments of a situation or person or self lead to antagonistic relationships with people and events. They place the judge in the position of winning and the one judged in a position of losing. The power lies in the judge—to grant a reprieve or to condemn.

If the person, instead, focused on how that other behavior or attitude did not work well, did not lead to human happiness and well-being, then he or she would work to make it more useful. This leads to winners all around. No one is condemned. The person works to help the other become a winner, a more fully alive person.

You help your children, then, by pulling from your language and spirit especially the negative judgmental labels. When Jimmy teases Judy, talk about how that doesn't lead anywhere positive rather than say, "That's awful, or bad, or wrong." No, it simply doesn't work.

Stay focused on human growth, and deal with your children's inappropriate behaviors as blocks to that growth rather than wrong acts. When the children make the "bad-wrong-awful" judgments on others, jump in (not all the time) and talk about how the other person's behavior might be leading away from any growth and happiness. Then ask how the children can move toward growing in that situation. Again, realize that this will not always produce immediate results. You are planting seeds, slowly and gradually attempting to influence the way your children see and view themselves and their world.

The way your children think and believe largely determines their feelings and behavior. Practically, it creates and greatly affects their personality. Realistic and reasonable thinking allows children, parents and teachers to accept and tolerate the uniqueness of each other; it leads to joining forces in a cooperative way for what we all want—our own growth and happiness, and that of our children. Happy thinking!

Chapter 7

Leading Children Toward Responsible Behavior

The opposite of responsible behavior is irresponsible behavior. For years we have called this "misbehavior." So, when parents and teachers say they want their children to "grow up to be responsible" they generally mean that they wish the children to behave appropriately in society. How you can aid your children making the choices for appropriate societal responses is the thrust of this chapter.

First of all, it would be extremely helpful to us as parents and teachers to attempt to view children's inappropriate behaviors as experiments in discovering how to belong and how to function in personally fulfilling ways, rather than to think of it as misbehavior. This different point of view simply helps us approach children's inappropriate behavior in a fresh way. If a child is "misbehaving," then punishment seems the logical response. If the child is "experimenting with ways of belonging," then guidance seems the more logical response.

A second important awareness in working with children's behavior involves our realization that the entire family unit acts as a system, and we all play a role in each other's behavior. When a child is brought to me with a "behavior problem" I want to know:

1. what the child does specifically,
2. what the parents and/or other family members do in response,
3. what the child does in reaction to the other person's response.

We, as parents and teachers, play a special role in our children's behavior. We keep their behaviors alive by the way we respond. For example, your son says, "Good night. See you in the morning." You say in return: "Good night. See you in the morning." Your response keeps your son saying the same thing every night. If you want him to stop saying that, then you would change your response. Perhaps you'd start saying: "No, Jim, I'll see you at midnight before I go to bed." Eventually Jim would most likely change his statement to: "Good night. See you at midnight."

Inappropriate behavior works the same way. The child yells and screams to get her way. The parents do not like that behavior. They want it to stop, so they get angry with the girl and scold her. She yells more. The parents yell more. Uproar ensues. The parents, in this case, are as much a part of the "misbehavior" as the child is. They keep it alive. Their upset reinforces the child's yelling behavior. If the child is seeking attention, the parents' yelling gives it to her dramatically. If the girl wants power, she gets it by watching the parents lose control of their own emotions right before her eyes. If the child wants to show the parents how inadequate she is, she accomplishes that when the parents throw up their arms in frustration and say "What can we do with you?"

The child → Parents yell → Child gets attention. Likes it.
yells.   back.   Yells again the next time
                                 something comes up.

There you have a system, all the parts of which are necessary to keep each element operating in the same way. As long as child and parent both respond in their usual way, the child's inappropriate behavior will continue. Oftentimes anger, yelling, and threats are the primary responses that parents turn to when meeting their child's misbehavior. They know that these ways will not change the child's behavior, but parents do not know what else to do. Even if this method does not work, they still use it. At least parents can vent their frustrations and may get slight temporary results. But the pattern continues. The child still yells when she doesn't get her way.

To change the child's behavior effectively, the parents can change their response in order that their screaming does not reward the girl. In other words, if the parents want to change the child's behavior they are encouraged to change their behavior first. By altering their response they affect the entire system, including the child.

In baseball, if the center fielder decided to talk with the fans rather than play ball, all the other players would have to adjust their play to continue the game. The whole system changes when one element changes. When one part of our car doesn't work we often say: "Our *car* isn't operating correctly." We make the statement about the whole machine. It would be equally helpful to see family life the same way. When one element doesn't seem to be working well, we might try to realize that "the family isn't operating well." That kind of thinking expands the possibilities for creatively dealing with teaching children to act responsibly and appropriately.

In any system the elements within it will resist change. This is particularly true in the family life system. If the parents decide to change their reactions to the children's behavior, the children will fight to get the parents back to the old way. Even if it seems evident that the new changes will lead to everyone's benefit, children (and adults) will often struggle to "get things back to normal," i.e., the way it was. And to get it back to "the old way" children will generally intensify their inappropriate behavior to convince the parents that their changes won't work. The parents often discourage very quickly, saying, "Well, that was a nice idea, but it doesn't work with my kids." And back they go to yelling and screaming.

Once, while working with a family, I encouraged them to set up a new system of behavior, that is, a new way of dealing with each other. The seven year old boy announced after the presentation of the plan: "It won't work. I can outlast all of you." Now that discouraged the parents right away. After considerable support from me, they went ahead with the plan, keeping in mind my warning: "The child's behavior will get worse before it gets better."

When I first began working with families, a set of parents brought in their eight year old son, complaining he would not go to sleep at night gracefully. At 8:00 P.M. he would begin throwing a temper tantrum that just wouldn't quit. The only way he'd go to sleep was if his father would bring the cot up from the basement and lay down alongside of his boy. After the boy fell asleep the father was then free to get up and continue his evening activities. If the boy awoke at 2:00 A.M. and the father was not lying next to him, Bruce would cry hysterically until father got out of his own bed and returned to the cot alongside Bruce's bed.

The parents were desperate . . . and exhausted. They had no idea what to do, so they continued doing what they were doing, even though they knew it wasn't working.

The dynamic was clear:

Bruce pitches fits.	→	Parents yell, scream, hit, give in, sleep next to him, etc.	→	Next night Bruce does the same thing all over again.

Bruce behaved this way for attention. And he received it in bushels. That reinforced his fits and tantrums. He learned that by behaving this way he got his parents' attention. His "misbehavior" worked. So he kept it up.

In order to break this pattern we look first to the parents' responses and invite them to change. In this case, the parents were instructed to totally ignore Bruce once the clock struck 8:00 P.M. He literally no longer existed for his parents. His behavior would get worse, but the parents were to grit their teeth and hold their own. It would get better, I assured them.

Little did I realize how persistent Bruce would be in attempting to force them to return to their former ways. That night as 8:00 P.M. approached Bruce began his routine—first whining about going to bed, then crying, then temper outbursts. When no response came from his parents, he intensified the action. He screamed, threw things in his room, and banged on the walls. Still nothing from the parents. They only turned up the TV a little louder. Bruce then came out of his bedroom and into the living room. He sat directly in front of the TV, blocking the parents' view. They said nothing, but picked him up and moved him. He presented a running commentary throughout the TV program.

Around 10:00 P.M. Dad and Mom were wearing a little thin. So Mom went grocery shopping at an all-night store and Dad went out to the garage to do some work. Bruce watched TV . . . for a while. Then he came out to the garage and tried talking with Dad. Dad refused to notice him. Around 11:30 Mom came home from the store and Bruce lassoed her around the waist with a rope and tied the other end to himself. That way he could follow Mom around wherever she went. At that point Mom wanted to junk this approach and pay attention to Bruce with anger. But she decided to tough it out.

Around 2:00 A.M. Dad and Mom went to bed. Bruce was still up, roaming the house. Around 4:00 A.M. the parents heard Bruce finally go to bed. At 6:00 A.M. the alarm went off. Time for Bruce to get ready for school. Of course he was in no condition to attend school. He felt sick and wanted his mother to call the school and excuse him for the day. Mother wisely told him that it was his problem and he should place the call. He did and announced to the principal: "I won't be coming to school today because I had a very rough night last night."

Bruce had to stay in his bed all day. Of course he slept all morning, but even in the afternoon when he felt fine, he had to remain in the position of a sick child with lights out, shades pulled, and no toys or games available. He just lay there. Around supper time he was allowed to get up.

Soon it was 8:00 P.M. again. The parents steeled their minds and bodies for another encounter with Bruce. They told Bruce it was bedtime and awaited his outbursts. Nothing happened. Bruce went into his room, said good night to his parents, and went directly to bed . . . and to sleep.

Bruce continues to go to bed without incident. He sorely tested his parents' new behavior, and discovered that he could not get the pay-off he wanted—their attention—by acting inappropriately. He learned that throwing tantrums was no longer going to get him attention from his parents. So he gave up throwing tantrums.

Bruce knew in the initial counseling session that his parents were going to totally ignore him from 8:00 P.M. on. He knew that no one was happy with the way things had been going at home. But simply talking about it didn't help. Bruce had to *experience* the fact that his inappropriate behavior was not a worthwhile enterprise for him to continue. Bruce learned that his irresponsible behavior no longer worked. It paid for him to act responsible.

Thus, to teach children to act responsibly, parents and teachers need to do two things:

1. Try to view the children's inappropriate behavior as an experiment in living rather than as misbehavior.

2. Realize that you will teach responsible behavior best by the way you react to the children's actions. Talking to them about irresponsible behavior will not teach as effectively as *acting* in relation to them.

Teaching Kids Consequences

Children can learn how to make personally responsible choices through their misbehavior. To do so they need help. And that's where you come in as parents and teachers.

When you operate out of an authoritarian style of parenting or teaching you do not allow your children to have choices. If they cannot have choices, they cannot learn to become independent thinkers, which is what most parents and teachers want for their children. Parents and teachers who think *for* their kids do a great disservice. When they answer the child's question "Why?" with "Because I said so," then they clearly restrict the child's independent thinking. These are the very parents and teachers I often hear complain about their children simply "following the crowd" and "not thinking for themselves."

For children to function in an independently responsible manner they need some freedom to make their own decisions.

The kinds of choices children need to have are not simply what flavor ice cream do they want or what color shirt to buy, but the very choice to behave appropriately or inappropriately. They need the freedom to misbehave if they are to learn personal responsibility. You read that correctly. Parents and teachers must literally give the child permission to choose behaving or misbehaving if that child is to gain a sense of responsible functioning in society.

By granting such permission, not only does the child get the opportunity to practice his decision-making skills for responsible behavior, but parents and teachers also reduce much of their anger regarding misbehavior. If you really believe that your children can learn best by experiencing the results of inappropriate as well as appropriate behavior, then you will view misbehavior as a process of learning. And if you, in fact, give the child permission to misbehave, then you will not be internally insisting that it should be any other way. That awareness will significantly reduce your anger with your children.

Now to the nuts and bolts. How do you teach responsibility through irresponsible behavior? Basically there are four steps:

1. Parents or teachers give the child the *choice* to behave appropriately or inappropriately.

2. Parents or teachers determine what the possible choices are.

3. Parents or teachers determine the consequences of each possible choice.

4. Parents or teachers then help the child *experience* the consequences of whatever choice the child makes.

Four year old Joan is not eating her supper, and instead is goofing around at the table. The parent gives the child a choice and means it. The parent also determines what the choices are from which Joan has to choose. Mom says: "Joan, you can either eat your food or not eat your food. It is your choice." Mom then determines the consequences flowing out of those two choices. She says: "If you eat your food, then you can have dessert. If you don't eat your food, you cannot have any dessert. It is your choice." That's it. No more talking. No more nagging about eating all her food. When dessert time comes, Mom helps Joan experience the consequences of her choice. If she ate her food, Mom gives her the dessert; if she didn't eat her food, Mom withholds dessert much to Joan's chagrin.

The child *chooses* a behavior *and chooses* the consequences of the behavior. The parent sets up the choices and the consequences; and then, after the child's choice, the parent helps the child experience fully the consequences of the choice.

Another example: Nine year old Joey often nags and whines and cries when he doesn't get his way. The parents would like such behavior to stop and they would like Joey to learn more responsible behavior. Here's how it works:

STEPS	CHANGE JOEY'S WHINING
1. Parents give Joey the *choice* to behave or misbehave.	They say: "Joey, it is your choice."
2. Parents determine what the possible choices are.	They say, "Either you talk calmly and reasonably or you continue whining and nagging."
3. Parents determine the logical consequences for each choice.	The consequence of calm and reasonable talk is that the parent can more easily receive the child's message and communicate with the child. In other words, communication takes place when both parties are presenting themselves rationally and sensibly. The consequence of whining and nagging and crying is that the parents find it very difficult to receive such

STEPS

CHANGE JOEY'S WHINING

messages and oftentimes become irritable in return. As long as Joey keeps up the nagging he is incapable of receiving any messages from his parents. Thus, the real consequence of Joey's behavior is a breakdown in communication. When communication has broken down, parents and Joey are wasting time with each other and should simply stop dealing with the other at that moment. So, the parents say: "Joey, if you talk calmly and reasonably now, I'm happy to continue our conversation. If you continue whining and nagging, I simply will not communicate with you at this time. It's your choice."

4. Parents help child experience the consequences of his choice.

If Joey stops whining and talks reasonably, the parents continue a dialogue with him. If Joey whines on, the parents totally ignore Joey and go on with whatever they are doing.

Let's go through the steps individually.

Step 1: Parents or teachers give the child the *choice* to behave appropriately or inappropriately.

Something inside of you needs to happen here. You want to believe that your child can make a free decision to act in any way possible. If you can recognize that children's misbehavior serves an important function in their growing up, then you can more effectively work with your children's actions. Children's misbehavior holds a key to teaching them how to make responsible choices.

Step 2: Parents or teachers determine what the possible choices are.

You, as the authority, operate here. You present the limits within which your children can decide. Usually the choices are an "either-or" type—"Either you do this or you don't do this." "Either cut the grass or don't cut the grass." "Either take a bath or don't take a bath." Most of the time you will be presenting directly opposite choices to your children. And generally those two choices arise spontaneously in you. Occasionally you will clearly exclude any other possibilities. "Either you can go to the ball game with the guys or you can stay home." You excluded as a possibility the party at Frank's house while his parents are out of town. As the parent with authority, I believe that you can exclude those choices that appear clearly harmful to your children.

Oftentimes the exclusion of a choice becomes the basis for a confrontation between you and your child. The only reason you have excluded a particular option is because your child wants that option. So you still have an either-or situation: "Either you do what I think is acceptable (stay home or go to the ball game) or you do what I consider unacceptable (go to Frank's party)." So, as parents, you always set up the choices. You make them as clear and distinct as possible. Now you are ready to tack on the consequences of the child's choice.

Steps 3 & 4: Parents or teachers determine the logical consequences for each choice and help the child *experience* those consequences.

Here comes the creative part of parenting—trying to discover the logical consequences of your children's behavior. What is the consequence of my five year old daughter playing with things on my desk while I write this (which is exactly what she is doing)? I ask her not to and to leave the den until I complete this chapter. I set up the options and the consequences for her: "Amy, either you leave the den until I'm finished or you don't. If you leave, I'll swing you on the swing when I am finished. If you don't leave right now, I'll take you to your room where you will stay until I do finish. It's your choice." Happily, she left without a complaint or a tear. It worked!

She is now bothering her mother. And I hear her mom setting up the choices and the consequences. It worked again! Now Amy is very quiet. I don't hear her at all. What is she up to? Excuse me while I check. She's much too quiet.

Anyway, thinking up the consequences of misbehavior can be pleasant entertainment when done with other parents. Let's look at typical "misbehaviors" and what the consequences might be:

Behavior	*Indicates*	*Consequences*
1. Temper tantrums	inability to communicate effectively	Communication breaks down, so I ignore child's yelling and cease talking in return.
2. Children fighting	inability to be together	I separate them to opposite corners of the house where they sit in isolation.
3. Little children riding bike in road	unawareness of possible danger and harm, as well as irresponsible use of bike	A physical pain is created by spanking rather than by collision with a car; and/or having bike taken away for a time; or having child brought into the house for a period of time.

Behavior	Indicates	Consequences
4. Getting up in time for school	inability to handle time in a responsible way	For every minute the child remains in bed in the morning, she will have to go to bed three minutes earlier in the evening. Or (if possible) let her miss the school bus and don't take her by car.
5. Not doing homework	poor use of time for important needs	Determine how much time the child would normally spend on homework; then each afternoon he spends that time sitting at the dining room table whether he does anything or not until he shows responsible action regarding homework.
6. Spilling things at table	irresponsible use of food and dishes and/or simply an accident	A mess is created. You instruct your child to clean it up. If it was an accident, you may help child. If irresponsible, the child may also be sent away from the table.
7. Little children getting into things while you are on the phone	an awareness that they can "get away with mur-	Whenever you are on the phone in the future, your child must immediately go to the corner chair and sit

Behavior	Indicates	Consequences
	der" at that time and have the freedom to misbehave	there until the phone conversation is over.
8. Stealing in the house	lack of respect for others' belongings	The child must return what was taken; or you may take from the child (with his or her knowledge) some material belonging he or she values for a period of time.
9. Staying out past curfew or leaving the house without informing parents as to where child is going	lack of responsibility in dealing with freedom in the social arena	Here, of course, grounding is the consequence.
10. Children failing to do expected chores around the house	unwillingness to cooperate in the normal functioning of the house	You can do the chores for your children and charge them for services just as you would pay a maid to clean house and cook meals.

In all the examples above the consequences are intended to stimulate your thinking. The best consequence must be created according to the situation and the child involved. Sending a child to her room which is stashed with TV, stereo, telephone, etc., will certainly not be an effective consequence for fighting with her brother. You know your child well enough to know what will cause her some hardships in order to help her react more responsibly in the future.

I want to give you a fuller explanation of example 10 above: children who don't do chores around the house that are expected of them. The logical consequences here work best for older children who place some value on money. It also assumes that the child has some source of income, either allowances or babysitting or paper route, etc. Let's say the chore is taking out the garbage every night. Paul, who is thirteen, always needs reminding. If his parents don't keep after him each day, he "forgets." Now, Dad and Mom do certain chores around the house, sister Beth does chores, and Paul is supposed to do some, too. If they all assume their responsibilities, the household runs efficiently. But what would happen if Mom stopped cooking and cleaning, or Dad stopped changing the oil in the car (or vice versa if the couple decides)? The work would not get done, and people would have to be hired or brought in to perform these tasks. In other words, the work that Dad and Mom don't do would have to be purchased.

The same applies to the children. If they do not do their tasks, the consequence is not an irate parent, but the children's experience of paying for services they *choose* (there's that word again) not to do. So, if Paul chooses not to take out the garbage at the appropriate time, Dad or Mom will do it, and simply charge him for their service. The fee for the chore is determined by the parents, based on the amount of income Paul brings in. They want to make the fee stiff enough so Paul feels it and would rather take out the garbage than pay the fee.

In presenting this arrangement the parent might say: "Paul, either you take the garbage out or you do not take it out. If you take it out, you will help us and help create a cooperative and happy atmosphere in the house. If you don't take it out, I will do it for you as a service. But I expect to be paid for that service, just as I would have to pay a maid or a cook to do my chores if I decided not to do them. So, each time I take out the garbage, I will charge you fifty cents. It is your choice."

You might also indicate the time at which the garbage is to be out and that you will only remind him one time a night. This strategy has been most effective in helping parents help their kids to function responsibly.

An observation about allowances. I do not believe that the granting of an allowance should be tied to children doing or not doing jobs around the house. I believe that some spending money is simply a part of life today, and that children should have some money on their person, just as a spouse not working outside the home should have money available. Thus, the granting of an allowance is not held over children to get them to perform. It is simply there as part of this family life.

However, if Paul refuses to pay his bill, then you can "garnish" his allowance. The next week you only pay him fifty cents instead of his usual two dollars because you took out the garbage three times.

Perhaps the major pitfall in attempting to teach responsibility in this fashion has to do with consistency and discouragement. Because the children want you to go back to the way you were responding before, they will give you the impression that your new approach doesn't faze them. When Mom explains to Paul that she will be charging for her services, Paul might respond: "Great! Then you'll be my servant and I'll pay you. No problem."

Do not become discouraged by that response. And do not change the response. Accept the child's statement and then carry out the consequences as you set them up. And *continue* to carry out the consequences. Do not revert to the old pattern because logical consequences "didn't work" right away. Stay with it for several weeks. Then if the desired results have not yet been achieved, keep the same consequences and add to them. If you revert to the former style, the children win the game and you remain as frustrated as before.

If the consequence you impose does not seem to work, then you may have a consequence that is reinforcing the inappropriate behavior, and is not experienced as a hardship at all. Then you can change the consequence.

Remember, hang in there. The child's behavior may get worse before improving. The dawn following the darkness, however, will be worth the struggle.

Principles in Teaching a Child To Act Responsibly

1. Give your child the *choice* to behave appropriately or inappropriately.

2. Then you determine what the possible range of choices is.

3. Create consequences for each possible choice.

4. Finally, help your child experience the consequences of whatever choice he or she makes.

5. Stick to it. Don't give up after two or three times. Keep in mind that your child's inappropriate behavior may get worse before it gets better.

Chapter 8

Helping Children Engage Life Fully

Neurosis happens when people deny a certain part of reality, psychosis occurs when people deny all of reality, and strong mental health takes place when people look at, acknowledge and engage all of reality. If you want your children to grow up psychologically sound, then you will want to teach them the skill of engaging life in all its aspects.

Your children engage life when they are open to hear your point of view; they deny it when they close off any input you have. They engage life when they continue playing a game even if they are losing; they deny it when they quit as soon as things do not go their way. They engage when they tell the truth; they deny reality when they lie. They engage when they are able to cry over hurts; they deny when they hold back the tears of disappointment. And so on.

The stance of an engaging child is one who continually *moves into* life's experience. Young Andy deals with what's in front of him. "This is the real world and I want to live in it, accepting whatever it has to offer" is the attitude with which he approaches daily living. He wants to test out life and live it as fully as possible. He chooses not to back away, not to make believe the world isn't there.

One of the best examples of the difference between engaging and denying stances occurs in the classroom. The teacher asks a question and no one is really sure of the answer. Moments of silence follow as the teacher waits for a student to raise his or her hand. As she looks around the room many children quickly look away from her, casting their eyes on their books or on the floor. Some children (not many) might continue looking at her. Those who look away are taking a tiny stance of denial. They believe, somehow, that if they do not see the teacher, then the teacher cannot see them. They deny the reality. Those who continue looking at the teacher show a tiny stance of engagement. They accept the reality before them: the teacher asking a question, they not knowing the answer. That's reality. It does not go away by closing eyes or looking away. (Adults do the same thing oftentimes. If I ask for a volunteer to demonstrate something while giving a talk, a number of people will look away and hope I cannot see them if they do not see me. That's a little denial in their life.)

Normally, children and adults are not totally engagers or deniers. Most of us have some of both sides. In certain areas we engage easily; in others we tend to deny. Let's take a look at the qualities of engagers and deniers. Then I'll talk about ways to help your children engage more fully.

1. Past/Future vs. Present

Deniers focus on the past and/or future. They are still upset tonight about what happened this morning. They let the past or future invade the present. Thus, they lose the fullness of the present moment. Children tend not to focus on past situations. They seem to naturally live in the present. That is a quality of an engager. Your children spontaneously and naturally engage the present rather than the past. They only learn to dwell on the past when we as parents turn back the clock of time.

2. Negative vs. Positive

Deniers focus on the negative dimensions of a situation; the Engagers notice the positive. In almost any of life's events pluses and minuses exist. The Engagers recognize both sides, and then attend to and enjoy the positive. The Denier says, "I'll never get another date." The Engager says, "I learned something from that experience. I'd rather go out with Jim from now on." The denying parent sees the big B among fine A's on the report card; the engaging parent sees fine big A's surrounding and overshadowing a very healthy B.

3. Force vs. Love and Reason

Deniers rely on force to get their way; Engagers use love and reason. Force or dictatorial authority is a way of negating or denying any other position. When parents or teachers use force as a general style of dealing with children, they effectively tell their children: "Your view or world does not exist. Only my world is valid and you must fit into it." The children, then, are thrown into a position where they must defend themselves and attempt to invalidate the parents' views. That style of non-acceptance of other views generates a stance of denial and intolerance of other people's beliefs and behaviors.

Engaging parents and teachers, on the other hand, seek to move into their children's world and beliefs. They respect the children's views, even if they might disagree with them. They figure that dialogue, couched in a respect for one another's opinion, might lead to new growth for everyone. They are not so committed to their own view that all their children must believe as they do.

These engaging parents and teachers seek to *move into* their children's minds, values, and attitudes. They accept that the values and thoughts are there, so they want to know and understand them. That way the parents and teachers might learn; also only when they know the thinking of their children can they influence their thinking and valuing in a positive way. The spirit of engaging parents and teachers is to get inside the workings of the children, no matter what they think or do. And then from the inside, they attempt to effect any changes through love and reasonable conversation. That's dealing with reality as it is, rather than the way we demand it must be through our use of dictatorial authority.

When Ann says she wants to see the R-rated movie, can you *enter* her thinking rather than jump right in with your opinion, thus denying her view? When Jason no longer wants to go to

Sunday school, can you move into *his* struggle rather than automatically negating his way of thinking and the conclusion he comes to? Then you are engaging.

4. Certainty vs. Risk

People who need absolute certainty about a situation before they can act will tend to limit the width and breadth of their lives. If reasonable risk is not part of their lives, they will rarely experience the ever-newness of life. They will become rigid, tight, ultra-conservative and cautious. Their bodies will show that internal imprisonment. They will be lifeless, tense, pale in color, cold, and somewhat distant. That almost sounds like the description of a dead person. Obviously, this is the stance of a denier.

The Engager risks. She will try new things, go to new restaurants, explore new relationships, stay open to new knowledge. She continually attempts to expand the horizons of her life. That kind of expansion leads to growth. And an Engager keeps growing more lively.

Denying parents and teachers demand certainty about their children. Parents, overly-cautious with their youngsters, teach them not to risk, to always play it close to the vest. Often, with first children, parents tend to be more cautious and careful. They become very protective of that first prize. "Be careful," "Watch out" and "Don't get too close to the edge" are phrases that may get over-worked by young parents. When this overly cautious style continues, then children learn the style of deniers—lay back, always play it safe, don't try anything new, keep up the same routine, etc.

The other place where you might slip into a denying stance is in "checking up" on your older children. I am somewhat surprised at the number of teenagers who complain to me about parents calling their friends to find out what their sons and daughters did last night. Parents who interrogate their teens as soon as they enter the house also display this need for certainty that signals a denier. Of course, some questions are appropriate, but the style is destructive when it demands more and more detailed information. Showing care and concern by an Inquisition style of questioning only leads to death in the relationship. It also teaches the child that it is best to shut up and not reveal much to others. That learning leads to interpersonal death.

Actually, there is very little certainty in *life*. In death there is certainty. Remember the old saying: "The only two things certain in life are death and taxes." As parents, you do not need *all* the facts to work with your children. Some information, yes. But every detail need not be spelled out. Too rigid a control over the details of a child's life can easily be experienced as very oppressive and suffocating to children. Their response will be to clam up and give even less information, and/or to lie as a way of avoiding your need for certainty.

The engaging parent allows the children to own their own worlds, and stands alongside them to understand and consult. That can be a little risky. The denying parent invades the heart and soul of the children's worlds and demands to know all. That is very risky, in fact, because it easily drives the children away from the parents. And who knows what it drives them toward?

5. Guilt vs. Non-Guilt

The Denier lives with guilt; the Engager lives with the normal limitations and mistakes of human beings. What makes guilt an act of denial is its focus on the past and on the negative. The guilty person looks at what he did yesterday and attends to the mistake; then he puts himself down for it. That leads to a denial of self as a worthwhile, life-giving person who has only this present, expansive moment of life. Guilt keeps him from entering fully into this moment.

The Engager admits mistakes, but then lets them die in the past, and focuses in a non-blameful way on the present. Parents and teachers who engage life do not hold grudges against their children. Once the mistake is over, it is over. To continue grumbling or displaying displeasure tells the children that past issues must continue for a long time into the present and future. Consequently, children get the idea that they should sustain bad feelings about past events. That leads to guilt. No, the past is past; in the present there is life and hope and the great possibility for change.

Children live easily in the present. How often have you corrected your children, only to have them retort immediately: "Dad, how come glass breaks?" Children quite naturally let go of past events. Guilt invades their lives when we live in the mistakes of yesterday, and when we tell the children how disappointed and hurt we are when they "do wrong." I suspect that is why children of divorce often blame themselves for the breakup of the marriage. They think that their parents are angry and hurt because of something the children did.

Guilt is generally not a useful emotion. It rests as a heavy burden on the child. More often than not it depresses children and stops them from "trying harder." And, of course, it seriously affects their self-image in a negative way.

Teaching Engagement

With engagement, we focus more on a *spirit* than a particular technique. When children are engaging, we sense it rather than observe and analyze it. We feel injected with life by these kinds of children. Consequently, the best teaching method is the engaging spirit of the parents and teacher. If you are Engagers and not Deniers, chances are that your children will also move into and not away from life.

Thus, modeling is the first and best method of teaching engagement to children. You can increase your own engaging behavior by checking those times and situations where you passively allow your life to live upon you rather than living life to your fullest in an active way. Make a list of those situations where you feel rather empty and restless when the time is over. Then see how you might shoot some of your own life into those occurrences.

My wife and I noticed that in the late afternoon of winter Sundays in Wisconsin we'd be ready to explode. Our children were restless, and we were annoyed and irritable. We detected a pattern: get up Sunday morning, go to church, eat brunch, read the newspaper, watch the football games and play some with the children. By 5:00 P.M. we felt lifeless. We realized that we kept our Sunday clothes on. That was the key. Whenever we wore good clothes, we tended to sit around. Good clothes are for sitting and visiting. We couldn't do too much, especially with young children, because we would get our clothes dirty. So we decided that after breakfast we would change into Saturday kind of clothes. We have been amazed at how delighted and rewarding our Sunday afternoons have become. We get outside and work a little and play a little. We do some jobs in the house, and play more "floor games" with the children. One little change (of clothes) turned us from Deniers to Engagers on Sunday afternoons.

If you look for those pockets of denial in your life and attempt to energize them, your children will experience a style of living that is upbeat and dynamic.

A second thing you can do as parents and teachers is respond quickly and immediately to daily situations. I'm talking about procrastination here. When you procrastinate with your children, you teach them to put off little pieces of reality.

Your young daughter asks you to read a book to her while you are reading the paper. You have two options: (1) either tell her "later," or (2) put down your paper and read to her. If you want to teach engagement, I believe that the second choice will be the more effective teacher.

Certainly, I am not suggesting that you always respond immediately to your children's requests. At times, when you are really engaged in a project (such as writing this book!), you may well teach engagement by the way you give yourself over to the task at hand. However, many times, when you delay responding to a request from the children, you will not be seriously engaged in something else. At those times, a quick, spontaneous response tells them about engaging life.

I would suggest that you model quick responses in other dimensions of adult life. When a light burns out, replace it immediately. It takes sixty seconds. When your spouse calls you and the children to supper, come right away. Pick up the dishes as soon as supper is over. Return the phone call as soon as you get the message. That spirit and style of responding to life's events as they appear before you signals a lifeful, energized person. Teaching by responding quickly models engagement to your children.

A third way of teaching engagement is through honesty. Being truthful means dealing with reality as it is. That is engagement. You face the world before you and present yourself as you are before the world.

If your company smokes and it irritates your eyes and stinks up the house, the engaging thing to do is let them know what is going on for you. If you just got home from work and the phone rings for you and you don't want to talk with anybody right now, your spouse need not say, "Oh, he's not home yet." That's a denial of reality. The engaging stance is to say: "He's just home from work. Can I have him call you back later tonight or tomorrow during the day?" That type of style tells your children that you deal with life as it is before you without attempting to manipulate it.

Honesty leads to a fourth way of teaching engagement, namely expressing your *feelings* directly to your children. The parents or teachers who move into life move as well into their emotions. They do not deny them, nor judge them as good and bad. They simply accept them as part of their life. And they share their feelings with their children—not all of them, but those the children can handle.

Anger seems to be a feeling most parents do express easily to their children. But they do not share many other emotions as gracefully. Anxiety, fear, sadness, disappointment, peacefulness, happiness, and joy are not as readily revealed to children. To present the whole range of your feelings indicates to them that you engage your emotions. And that can teach children to move into and not away from their own feelings.

I think that children can handle their mother's worry about inflation or their father's fear of riding on a roller coaster. They can learn to accept their parents' disappointment over some significant loss. And they are able to acknowledge their parents' happiness and love for them.

The regular expression of feelings by parents to their children allows young people the opportunity to treat emotions as a normal and common aspect of life. They will learn not to be afraid of their feelings, and so will not deny them. They will engage, instead, one of the most significant dimensions of human life—their feelings.

A fifth way of teaching engagement is through receiving the thoughts, values, behaviors, and feelings of your children. By acknowledging their feelings and beliefs in a non-judgmental way, you say to your children: "I engage with you your reality. I do not deny that it exists or that you exist. I respect your existence and I enter it." You may disagree with your children's rule, but you still engage it.

Nothing so scares engaging parents that they are not willing to look at it. If their children bring something to them, be it a field mouse or a thought, these parents attend to it. At times the thoughts and values that your children present may strongly differ from your own. Rather than attempt to save your children from those destructive thoughts, can you try to enter them, see them from the inside, and acknowledge their point of view? Later, you can disagree. But first engage the *children's* thoughts and values. Be willing to go on journeys of the mind with them. You do not have to stay at the same motel. But taking the trip through their mind tells them what it is like to engage all dimensions of life.

Finally, you help your children engage rather than deny by your own ability to be casual and keep your sense of humor. If everything you do or see becomes a serious, intense event that cannot allow for inconsistency and incongruity, you deny the real world.

Children spontaneously see the lightness of events. They laugh about things that don't seem funny at all to you. Engaging parents and teachers attempt to enjoy their children and see from their children's perspective. They do not deny their children the luxury of being children. They do not demand that the children become adults too quickly and "give up" the fun and "goofiness" of childhood.

For example, young children enjoy doing the same things over and over. That may not seem productive or interesting to us, but engaging parents see through their children's eyes and sense their enjoyment over reading the story "one more time."

Young children often like physical "rough-house" activity. They enjoy playing "tickle monster" or wrestling. The denying parent cannot enter something so silly; the engaging parent can.

Later, when the children are older, engaging parents and teachers sense a letting go and grant more independence. They do not believe that every word that comes from the teenager has to be taken as the child's final position. Actions and expressions of children are generally taken more seriously by parents than by the kids. I am not suggesting that we take nothing seriously from our children. I only want to warn against an over-seriousness that frustrated a child's light-hearted enthusiasm for life.

After giving a talk to a group of parents on this subject, a father approached me and shared his act of engagement with his teenage son. He hated the loud music his son listened to. He could not understand it, and tried to dissuade his son from "getting into it." Of course, his son thought that his dad was an old fuddy-duddy. They would argue about modern pop music's pluses and minuses.

The son kept saying that it was meaningful and that his dad simply did not give it a chance. So the father decided to engage his son's type of music. He told his son that he wanted to go to the next pop concert in the city. He promised not to sit with his son, if that would embarrass him.

They went to listen to some group I have never heard of. The father and mother (he pulled her along) tried hard to understand and enter the music. They thought that they succeeded partially. After the concert, they talked with their son and his friends about the music. While the father and mother did not become full converts, they had a new experience and a fascinating conversation with their son and his friends. The father reported that his son seemed to respect, even admire, him more because "he was open."

Perhaps most important, though, the parents modeled for their son the skill of engagement. They demonstrated their movement into life, even the possibility of life at a pop concert. By their action they told their son to stand open to all that might enrich him.

As you conclude reading this chapter I hope that you sense this spirit of engagement. *Moving into* the daily events of parenting and teaching wholeheartedly communicates to your children a zest and love for life. It demonstrates to your children a stance toward life that leads to good mental health, and it tells them that the most effective way to live is to engage all that is present to them, to enter life and not move away from it.

Chapter 9

Promoting Children's Decision-Making Skills

As parents and educators, we hope that our children will make choices throughout their lives that will lead to their own well-being and that of others. As these children enter their teen years, we worry that they do not simply "follow the crowd." We don't want them making choices solely on the authority or pressure of their peers. We want them to think critically and decide according to their own inner norms of love, reason, and justice.

Allowing for real decision-making by children, however, can be difficult for parents and teachers. Clinging tightly to the walls of our stomach is a fear that "all hell will break loose" if we really let them decide. We sense that they do not have the equipment or the experience to make the "right" judgment. We have traveled through life and know what is best for them. So, we believe, it is not in their best interest to let them decide the important issues.

Certainly, we cannot let three year old children decide to play in the street or not. And we will try very hard to stop our seventeen year old from getting married. Or we may insist, as educators, that kids cannot only study Pink Panther comic books in class.

I am not suggesting that we give our children total control over every life and school decision they have. But I am encouraging you as parents and teachers to move beyond the tokens of decision-making we offer them now.

We do not teach decision-making skills to children by giving them choice only in peripheral issues. Whether we go to Pizza

Hut or McDonald's does not develop decision-making power. Choosing which songs to sing at the school assembly also does not increase their decision-making ability.

Gradually, children in the home and school need to be involved in meaty decisions. At home that will mean where vacations are taken, rules for the upkeep of the house, ways of relating to each other, financial management of the household, and so on. At school it will mean having a voice in the development of curriculum, in how classes are conducted, in rules for discipline, in procedures for class interaction and so on.

Again I want to emphasize the gradual nature of these kinds of decision-making involvements of children. As responsible adults, we need not abandon our involvement in the decision-making process, since we have a great deal of information and experience to offer. But if our goal is teaching children decision-making skills, then that *process* becomes more important than most of the *contents* we deal with.

To engage children in real decision-making demands our willingness to risk that our way will not always be chosen by the children. When that happens, we may need to do more negotiating and discussing, and we may need to work harder to help our children learn the consequences of their decisions.

Often I hear parents and teachers *voice* a desire that the children learn to be decision-makers, but then not carry it out. By decision-making these parents and teachers mean "that process whereby the children decide what I think is best for them." I have caught myself entering this little dialogue with my children:

"Amy, do you want some peas?" Here's a question of choice. I am apparently giving her the option of selecting peas or not having peas for supper.

She says, "Yuk! I don't want any peas. They're terrible."

Then I respond: "Well, I think you should have at least some. They're good for you." And I plop two spoonfuls on her plate.

I gave her a choice; then I took it away. If you do not want the child to have a choice on a certain issue, then do not set up choices for her. Simply tell her that she is getting the peas. On the other hand, if you give choices, then be prepared to accept the decision of the child.

Another difficulty in teaching decision-making is our societal orientation of one person, one vote. Voting can reinforce a sense of helplessness in children if they lose the decision on some regular basis. They become cynical and say things like: "What difference does it make anyway?" Many adults feel the same way when it comes to civic elections.

Using voting as a decision-making tool in the home or school creates a win-lose situation. Win-lose can easily get translated into "right-wrong" for children. The next translation becomes "*I* am right" or "*I* am wrong. The majority is right; the minority is wrong. It is not good to be in the minority. Therefore, I will always try to side with the majority. I will follow the biggest crowd."

Voting, then, can reinforce the very thing we are trying to avoid, namely, going along with other people's choices. Generally, trying to work toward *consensus* will get better results for teaching decision-making skills. In this style, children and parents/teachers make input and jointly decide. This style will involve compromise and considerable flexibility on the part of the parent/teacher. But if you are earnest about teaching decision-making skills, then compromise and flexibility will serve you well.

An effective way of helping children process their decisions is by inviting them to answer questions about the choices they have, and then helping them frame the choices and see the consequences of both sides. But a big caution: Watch out for preaching or lecturing. Children don't listen to that. The method used by the philosopher Socrates when he taught seems to work best.

Here's a brief example of how this works. Tommy wants to get a baseball glove. To do so, he needs to save his money. But when he gets money he wants to buy baseball cards. He has trouble saving.

Tom: "Dad, why don't you just buy me a glove?"
Dad: "Why do you think you're having difficulty getting that glove?"

Tom: "Because I just can't save any money."

Dad: "I wonder why that is. You earn and get about two bucks a week."

Tom: "I don't know."

Dad: "Where do you think that two dollars goes each week?"

Tom: "Oh, I don't know. For stuff I need."

Dad: "For stuff you absolutely need or just like?"

Tom: "Well, it's junk I want to get."

Dad: "So you make a decision to get things you want right away. Somehow, getting those things right now is more important for you than getting a glove. Is that right?"

Tom: "No. I really want a glove. But I want that other stuff, too."

Dad: "So you want both a glove and other stuff even though you only have so much money. That's a problem, right?"

Tom: "I suppose."

Dad: "How do you solve the problem?"

Tom: "I don't know. I suppose I can't buy my baseball cards if I want a glove."

Dad: "In other words, you can't have both the cards and glove, huh? It seems as though you'll have to make a choice between the two. If you could only have one thing, the glove or the cards, which would you rather have?"

Tom: "The glove."

Dad: "So then you'd have to sacrifice the cards until you get the glove, right?"

Tom: "Right."

Dad: "So Tom, the choice seems to be either to stop buying the cards for a while so you can enjoy having a glove, or to keep buying the cards and enjoying them, but not have a glove. It's your choice, right?"

Tom: "Yeah, I guess so."

No lectures and no moralizing. Only an effort to help Tom clarify the choices and the effects of those choices. You leave the choice entirely up to him, because whatever way he decides, he will learn about the results of his choices. As his parent, you have stood with him in his dilemma and helped him clarify and reflect on his choices. That process is much more important than whether he gets a glove or baseball cards. Tom is learning critical thinking, a skill he needs to make sensible choices. The glove or cards will die in a very short time.

Another method of teaching decision-making to children is through the family or classroom meeting. Initially the meetings can be used more as a forum to air ideas and feelings than as a time to hammer out decisions. In this way children can get used to the idea of offering their thoughts in a group, while the parent or teacher need not fear a loss of control. Children and adults will need time to adjust to joint decision-making.

Perhaps the two qualities most needed by parents and teachers in order to help develop this decision-making ability in children are a curiosity for the truth and personal flexibility. The desire to know will help you to continually ask the questions. Generally, the more information you possess, the easier that decisions are made. To raise questions, to not accept something as true just because you heard it on TV, to request more evidence, to look up another source—these are healthy stances we communicate to our children about making decisions.

And flexibility! Most forms of rigidity stifle effective decision-making, because rigidity tends to cause tunnel-vision. When we lock ourselves in to view the world in only one way, we impoverish our choices. We only know how to drive to work this one way; we only know how to respond to our kids by yelling; we only know how to diet by starving, then stuffing; we only know how to pray by going to this church service. Habit limits our freedom to choose from a wide array of possibilities.

To do something because "it's always been done that way" stifles the possibilities for growth. If you always shop at one store because you have always shopped there, you may never notice all the different styles in other stores. I have been dealing with the same office machine store for seven years. This store has sold me typewriters and repaired them all this time. Therefore, when I needed a new office typewriter, I went back to the same place. I then told my wife what the typewriter I wanted would cost, and she suggested that I check a couple of other stores. I had never thought of that. I did check and found an even better machine for four hundred dollars less. Flexibility saves money, too!

An ability to move with the flow of our children's lives will help them in learning to make sensible decisions. Being flexible and open will allow them the freedom to explore the rich possibilities in their world. Again, I am not suggesting that we abandon our responsibility for their physical and psychological safety. But I am encouraging us to leave the other end of the continuum, which represents rigidity, stubbornness, narrow-mindedness, and habit-forming stuckness.

Kids will make unworkable decisions at times. Our task is to consult with them in their decision-making process, let them decide, and then be there for them if they need us after the fact. Fortunately, most of their decisions will not affect life and death matters. And if we have worked with them from early childhood in making sound choices, when the big decisions come, hopefully they will choose wisely for their growth and that of others.

Chapter 10

Teaching Children Religious and Moral Values

In family counseling, one of the most popular conflicts between parents and children arises over going to church on Sundays. The dialogue goes like this:

Kids: "It's so boring. I don't want to go."

Parents: "As long as you're part of this family you will go with us."

Of course the children win this battle even if they do have to go. You see, once they get to church they do not have to pray. You can get them in the pew, but you cannot force them to worship. Not only that, but they will sabotage your prayer also with their sighs, and grunts, and fidgeting.

Force does not make children value something differently. If you want them to value religion, forcing them to go to church hardly attains that goal.

I continue to insist that parents need to know and believe their own religious tenets and communicate these effectively to their children. To tell kids they have to go to church because they are members of your family fails miserably in helping them value their religion. They need to experience _your_ faith and understanding. As St. Paul said: "Faith comes through hearing." He did not say that it comes through force.

Unfortunately, many adults who happen to be parents and educators do not know their own faith sufficiently to communicate it to their children. This, then, is the starting point. To help your children value their religion, you must start with increasing your own knowledge through reading or adult education programs, and you must be willing to share your enlightened faith with your children.

Many texts and books have been written on instructing children in their faith. In this single chapter I cannot explain what and how religion should be taught. But I can share with you what I think children can grasp (adults, too) and some specific themes to highlight.

Teach God as Creator

In the first book of the Bible God is revealed as the *Creator*. This notion of God is most basic and simple. God is the one who creates. God sets it all in motion in one way or another. Once God creates, what has been created is allowed to develop to its own state of perfection.

God is not simply Creator, but loving Creator. In other words, God loved so fully that the result of that act of loving was the world and all creation. And because God continues this act of loving we are all held in existence. God did not create us and then love us because we turned out pretty nice. Rather, he loved and we are the results of that over-flowing act.

God as Creator does not mess around with our lives. We have been created with free will to become our best selves or not. Generally, God does not butt in, because if he did, we would no longer have free choice and consequently would cease being human.

So, in teaching children, we can continue to show them the loving creative energy of God in all of nature, and especially in human nature. We can teach them that by our free choice we can cooperate with this creative God in becoming our best selves, or we can choose not to cooperate, thus becoming less human.

God Is Known in the Human Condition

As human persons we *know* through out material bodies. We learn through our senses. If Jack is to know Jill, she must reveal herself (her inner spirit) through words and gestures. Jack picks these up and gradually comes to know Jill.

God, who we sense is fully spirit, can only reveal through the material he has created. Primarily, God reveals through people. More specifically, as people become more and more human by developing life skills, they reveal by their lives who God is.

For instance, when Jack and Jill really communicate in a giving and receiving way, they will experience a bondedness with one another. That union they sense also is the revelation of God. Through that human experience they now know God as united or bonded to them. When they feel loved, they know God the lover. When they feel free to make decisions, they know the freedom of God. When they go out of their way to assist someone else, they know the compassionate God.

<u>God is known, then, primarily in our own human experience</u>. This makes sense to kids. It does not make sense to kids that God is off on some cloud somewhere. God and religion need to be understood through children's human, day-to-day experiences and feelings.

Try Reconnecting the Bible

If we think of God as loving Creator, then we have some translating to do with the manner in which the Bible and Church teachings have come to us and our kids. We need to connect the Bible and Church teaching to human life experiences. What follows is an example of translating the Ten Commandments for kids. This appeared in a column on fathering I write in a weekly newspaper.

Loving Commandments

Our experiences as dads sometimes helps us to understand God our Father. This happened to me a while ago when I took my children to Baskin-Robbins for ice cream. To understand the revelation, you have to think of me, the father, sort of like God. And my children as my creation!

We walk in and I give them free choice to pick whatever flavor they want. But, because I know them so well, I know which flavors they would like and which they wouldn't. So Amy looks them over and decides she wants daiquiri ice. Now, I know she will not like daiquiri ice, and I tell her so. But she insists, thereby "breaking my will" for her happiness. However, since I gave her the choice, I must abide by her decision.

Of course, because I love her so much, and I see her making an unhappy choice, I must work a little harder to help her gain happiness. Her choice does not really offend me; it only leads to her disappointment. So, loving father that I am (!), I buy chocolate mint for me. Then, when she gags on the daiquiri ice, I switch cones, giving her my chocolate mint and eating her daiquiri ice (ugh!).

Now I understand better about Commandments and God's will. God's Commandments are much like my encouragement to Amy to choose a flavor she will enjoy. The Commandments were simply stated in harsher tones: "Amy, thou shalt not choose daiquiri ice." The Commandments could have been written the way I talked to Amy in Baskin-Robbins. Then they might have sounded like this:

"My sons and daughters, I am your loving father. Please trust that I will always care for you. Call me whenever you need me. I have so much to share with you. I hope you come often to visit.

"I can assure you, you will be very happy in life if you love others and try not to hurt them in any way. Respect and reverence for other persons will work better for you than using and manipulating them. Try to use things in the service of people and not the other way around. Although tough at times, being totally honest will bond you more fully to others. And work to enjoy yourself and what is yours, while celebrating others and what they hold dear for them.

"I, your father, tell you these things only because I know that they will work toward your happiness. But I have given you free choice, so it's up to you. <u>If you choose another way, it does not offend me, and I will not abandon you. No, instead I'll just have to work harder to help you reach fulfillment despite your sometimes goofy choices.</u>"

That's how I loved Amy in Baskin-Robbins one afternoon. And now I know that God my Father loves me every afternoon when I choose among all those flavors of life.

Teach the Natural Law

To teach moral principles to children assumes that we know what principles we use to determine right and wrong. Over the years I have had the opportunity to ask numerous people what principles they use to decide if something is morally right or wrong. I cannot remember anyone giving me a very clear answer. Most people admit they do not know, or have not ever thought about it. In order to teach your children, then, you need to become clear about how you determine right and wrong.

Ultimately, the norm for our behavior lies within us, in the depths of our very nature as human beings. The *natural law* is that law which states that we must live according to our nature. Living according to our nature means to live and function as *humanly* as possible. And practically, how do we live humanly? Be developing the kinds of skills we are discussing in this book. We live humanly when we communicate well, believe accurately about our world and ourselves, engage the reality of our lives, make responsible decisions, love one another, and bond as best we can to all the bits and pieces of creation. These stand as the elements of the natural law.

Expressed as clearly as possible, the natural law states: <u>Good is that which leads to human growth; evil is that which leads away from human growth</u>. All the other laws, Church and state, must somehow conform to this fundamental law of nature. Simply because they have been stated as laws does not put them in harmony with the law of our nature to be human.

Your own sense of clarity regarding this issue of conscience will assist you immensely in teaching your children a healthy moral sense.

Present a Wholistic View of Creation

Children often wonder how we all got started and where we all end up after death. What do you want your children to believe? That with death it's all over? That you can end up in heaven or hell? That you must do time before you get to heaven? That your hell is now and heaven comes later?

Let me share with you what I sense makes most sense to kids. Young people can relate well to theories of evolution. I think teaching them that we evolved out of some lower animal form into human creatures registers well with them. "Original sin," then, can be viewed as the choice of our first parents, in part, away from accepting full human growth. Instead, they regressed in the evolutionary process. That is, they chose to be less than human. (There again is the moral principle I discussed above. Sin or evil is the movement away from human growth.)

As a human species we continue to evolve in a self-correcting way that leads to a higher life form than we presently know. With our death we move into that next life form filled with more love and freedom (the two special traits of human beings). The symbol we have of this is the dying and rising of Jesus in the Bible.

Perhaps our best argument that we will evolve into a higher life form is our present human experience of love. Love possesses a *forever* quality about it. When we are loving someone, we are loving with time limits. Since that forever quality is present, it does not seem likely that it will be frustrated by death, but only be transformed into a fuller dimension.

Thus, the people we love and cherish here we will love forever and be with forever in whatever life (or lives) lie ahead of us.

Our purpose in life here, then, is to develop our humanness (our love and our freedom) in order to continue our evolution as persons and to continue cooperating in God's creative action in our lives.

My effort here has not been to present some complete theological treatise, but rather to share with you some views that seem to make sense to young people. Each of us as parents or educators needs to gain our own clarity regarding these large issues. Then out of that clarity and conviction we can hope to impart our faith and moral sense to our children.

Chapter 11

Encouraging Children Toward Healthy Sexual Attitudes

When I ask parents to do free association with the notion of sexuality related to their children, they say words like "safety, dangerous, scary, morals, touchy." Sexuality triggers a variety of reactions in parents, from guilt to permissiveness to embarrassment to comfortability. Often surrounded in secrecy, it leads to intense curiosity among children. It stands as the single area in parenting that is most avoided verbally with children, yet it is the topic most needful of adult input to these children.

For children to develop a healthy attitude toward sex, parents and teachers need to place it in a context of human development. If sex is taught as a single entity, separated from the whole dynamic of human living, it will be like studying the word "green" separated from the sentence "The trees are turning bright green in the springtime."

Recently a father complained to me about sex education in the public school system. He said: "They only teach the plumbing parts. They don't put it in the context of values and the expression of love."

I believe that sex is best taught to children in the context of humanness and love. The verbal conversation about sex will take on ever more power when the children experience their parents' love for one another.

Sexual activity accomplishes three ends:

1. It creates new babies.
2. It gives physical pleasure.
3. It expresses and intensifies love.

Traditionally and historically, different aspects have been highlighted. In the recent past, conceiving children appeared as the primary purpose of sex, especially in religious or church circles. At other times (now might be one of them) physical pleasure was highlighted as a central goal of sexual activity. Sex as the expression of real love seems to have played the role of handmaid or "also ran" to these other dimensions. It has always been there as a secondary statement. Yes, sex also expresses human love between people.

I believe, however, in teaching children about sexuality, we best serve them by making it clear that sex is *primarily* the expression of love that completes, reveals, and intensifies a loving bond between two people committed to each other's growth and development. It *also* is the way children are created, and it yields physical pleasure.

Like all other activities of human life, sex needs to lead to personal growth. It needs to be truly a human act. An action leads to humanness when it flows out of our nature, when it follows the laws of our nature (the natural law). And the fundamental notion of the natural law is to move toward being one's fullest and best self. That occurs when our outer self of feelings and behaviors matches our deep inner movements and energies. When sexual activity emanates from the deep inner movement of love, then it leads to human growth.

Sexual activity signals a union between two people in which the giving-receiving rhythm of communication has been established. When the spirit of love sparks the relationship, the dynamic of giving and receiving tends to move across the entire marriage. In words, actions and feelings the two partners give to and receive from each other the life-sustaining forces needed for growth. Sexual activity snuggles warmly into that same dynamic and becomes a rich moment of giving and receiving. It not only symbolizes the giving-receiving nature of the relationship, but it also gives impetus to deeper love between the spouses.

In our present age, sex is often pulled out of the context of love, and isolated as an entity unto itself. It signals, instead, the dimension of physical pleasure. Certainly, physical pleasure does not in itself dehumanize. On the contrary, our bodies naturally move toward pleasure. But when sex for physical pleasure gets so highlighted that it no longer is seen in the context of love, then it begins to dehumanize the people using it.

If you eat potato chips just for the pleasure they give, you *use* the chips. But chips are chips and that's that. When you *use* another person just for sexual pleasure, you make the other person an object (like the chips) to be consumed. But persons, made to grow, are subjects, not objects. When treated as such, they cannot be free to be fully alive with the whole range of feelings.

Human beings grow best when another relates to them in empathic and sensitive ways, surrounding them in love and care. To use an action naturally established to serve that end (as is sexual intercourse) solely for self-gratification damages the rhythm of true giving and receiving, and forces one person to attend to the other as "thing" rather than person. This dehumanizes both parties.

Thus, in attempting to teach children about sexuality, it is most effectively done in the context of a loving home environment. Here children can experience sexuality in the context of love. They will learn about it not only as a biological function, but as a full human act between two subjects, attentive to each other with respect and caring.

Almost any other mode of sexual education will be presented outside the context of love. Certainly when children learn about sex from their teenage friends it will not be surrounded in the notion of love. Finding out about sex in novels, television, or movies generally leads children to focus on the passion and physical dimensions of sex. Even the better sex education courses taught in schools and churches tend to stay with the physical dimensions of sexual activity. Public school systems, in particular, need to stay with factual information, and cannot teach much about values underlying sexual activity. So, you see, only in a loving home environment is sexuality most fully taught.

Teaching Sex at Home

In the atmosphere of a loving, giving-receiving home, you can do a number of things to help your children grow in an understanding and respect for their own and others' sexuality.

1. Show Children All Dimensions of a Marriage Relationship

First of all, you want to demonstrate to your children the fullness of the marriage relationship. They need to know that sex is only one element (and a relatively small one at that) in this multi-faceted bond between husband and wife. Children first have to understand that it takes energy and work to develop a growing relationship and that the sexual dimension fits in as the rest of the relationship intensifies and flourishes.

Practically, parents need to express feelings of love and tenderness to each other in front of the kids. Hugs and kisses between parents let children know that affection need not always be connected to sexual intercourse. Parents sharing common interests or differences or problems indicate to kids that the marriage bond develops in a wide variety of ways.

A most important bond that children need to see in their parents is humor and light-heartedness. If parents really *enjoy* each other, can laugh and joke, they teach their children that the most meaningful pleasure lies in the positive relationship, not in an isolated physical action. Sexual activity, however, is enhanced and made more pleasurable when the whole relation fills up with pleasure and joy.

In working with teenagers on sexuality, I have found one explanation that seems to help them understand sexuality better than others. In the beginning, sexual activity can so dominate a relationship that other elements of real friendship may never develop. Sexual intensity can cut off many of the threads that tie a relationship together between a boy and girl. Due to the force of sexuality, young people can be deceived that they have a relationship "born in heaven." They are convinced that the "little" differences they notice will be easily overcome by the intensity of their "true love." They are kidding themselves.

The "true and deep love" they experience may well be sexual infatuation and excitement. The young couple believes that the entire relationship is full and complete, but it isn't. It takes a long time for two people to really establish a full and deep love for one another. In fact, such a rich relationship happens far beyond the sexual aspect.

The true bonds of love lie in two people giving to and receiving from each other in the mutual understanding of their needs. The couple needs to bond on their interests, values, family histories, goals in life, beliefs about family, moral principles, personalities, psychic strengths and weaknesses, and so forth. If sex comes into the relationship too soon, it tends to dominate these other bonding elements and does not let them grow.

Then when the young couple marry they quickly realize that the sexual bond begins to modify and the relationship looks to the other bonding forces for strength. If those bonds are weak, the relationship often falls apart. No wonder that the majority of divorces occur within the first five years of marriage.

I then tell young people: If you really want to love this other person, and stay growing in love, then play down the sexual part of the relation and increase your focus on all the other bonds. Don't let sex become too important too quickly unless you don't care if you lose each other.

This explanation seems helpful to young people if they are presently not involved in a sexual relationship. They can make sense of it. If they are sexually involved with someone, they will not hear much of anything we have to say.

2. Explain Sex at an Early Age

Most children have asked all the questions by the time they are four. Most parents and teachers, however, have not answered all the questions when asked. The reason, I suspect, is that many adults are not comfortable talking openly about sex.

While I do not advocate pulling out the charts as soon as the toddler asks "Where did I come from?" I do believe that parents should answer that question using accurate terms and giving as much detail as the child can receive. If children hear words like penis and vagina when they are two, it won't be hard for you to say the words when they are twelve and fourteen.

Oftentimes those two words—penis and vagina—cause difficulty for adults. They just do not seem easy to say for many people. If that is the case for you, then I suggest that you practice saying them by having a conversation about sex with your spouse or a close friend. Getting comfortable with the words of sex can lead to ease in talking with children about sex.

What are some of the questions and responses that might arise between parent and young child (two to four years old)?

Where do I come from? You come from Daddy and Mommy.

How? You start to grow inside Mommy's uterus; and, then, when you get so big, you come out of a hole called a vagina between Mommy's legs.

But you said I come from Daddy too? Daddy helps by putting a little seed in Mommy's body, and then you grow up inside Mommy.

How does Daddy get the seed inside Mommy's body? (The big question!) Daddy puts his penis into the hole between Mom's legs, the vagina, and the seed goes from his penis into her vagina.

What's a penis? A penis is the part of a man's body between his legs that he uses when he goes to the toilet and pees (or urinates or whatever word you use here).

Does Dad pee into Mom's body? No, when Daddy puts his penis into Mom's body a special kind of liquid or water comes out that has seeds in it that can make babies. Inside Mommy is a little egg. When the seed from Dad and the egg in Mom meet, then that's the start of a wonderful new person. And the person we started was you.

Why do you do that anyway? Well, when Dad and Mom love each other so much we like to be very close. Sometimes we want to be so close we'd almost like to be right inside each other. Then we kiss and hug and get our bodies very close. To be even closer Dad puts his penis into Mom's vagina. We love each other very, very much at those times and enjoy being so close. Then some seed will go from Dad to Mom. So, you see, when we started making you it was because we were loving each other so much. And you are the gift of our love. Now, we love you a whole lot too.

And the child goes off to play with some toys, responding to that conversation no differently than to a discussion on why the sky is blue. I think it's wise to only answer the children's questions as far as they ask them. Usually, they won't ask all the above questions at once. If they are content with a simple, general answer, although accurate, that's fine. Do not elaborate if you do not need to. It only confuses them. Go as far as you need to.

3. Keep Young Bodies Active

Boredom happens to the mind *and* the body. When children would rather be somewhere else or be doing something other than what they are presently doing, they are psychologically bored. In the springtime, they would rather be playing outside, but they have to sit in the classroom. They get bored. When they feel bored, they get restless. So their minds drift and their ability to concentrate fails them.

Bodies also can become bored. The human body orients toward activity. It was not created to simply sit. It needs the stimulation of action. If it does not get that stimulation to satisfy itself, it seeks quick stimulants.

When the body becomes bored, it says to the person, "I don't like doing nothing. I need activity. I need blood charging through me. I need something going on inside." But not much is going on, so the body gets discouraged. It becomes apathetic, and begins looking for very quick and easy stimulators that will not take much energy.

For teenagers in our culture with bored bodies, some of the quick stimulants are loud music, drugs, alcohol, food, TV, cigarettes, and sex. (By the way, these same instant stimulators are used by adults with bored bodies.) When the human body misses out on vigorous and frequent activity, it seeks its satisfaction in whatever quick and easy means are available.

Because one of the fast stimulants for the bored body is sex, you can see how a child's sexuality will be drawn out of the context of loving and caring. It moves instead into a framework of "sex for bodily pleasure." This "educational process" diverts the child from the true meaning and use of sex.

I am not sure that parents can do much to alter this trend when discovered in teenagers. The pattern has been fairly well established. With younger children, though, parents can encourage more physical activity.

While athletic endeavors in themselves may not be a value to many parents, I personally believe that children involved in them greatly increase their overall physical and psychological development. I consistently see children who are involved in sports functioning in more mature ways than those not so involved. They give so much energy to these activities that their bodies seem not to need the other kinds of quick stimulants as much. In relation to sex, then, they tend not to focus on it so intently.

Strenuous, vigorous physical activity can serve as an important teacher in the area of sexuality. The body is less likely to seek sex out of context. Certainly, that does not mean that kids who play sports won't feel sexual and that kids who don't play sports will. It does mean, though, that parents will help their children in a variety of areas if they encourage and model physical action. This activity may help young people de-emphasize the focus on sexuality too early or too intently.

4. Find an Adult Friend

No matter how open and easy the communication between parents and children, sometimes talking about sex with parents seems very difficult for children. To cover that base, you might attempt to help your children get to know and feel comfortable with some other adult person to whom they might turn. Teachers can be very helpful here, also. Kids will often give subtle cues to teachers that they might want to talk about sex. Pay close attention to your students so that you can be there for them when they need the adult view on sexuality.

You want the person in whom the child confides to have your values, in general, and especially so in the area of sexuality. It might be a relative, neighbor, or close friend. Or it might be a contact the child has from school, church, or some other group. This adult might foster that relationship by taking your child to a game, concert or out to breakfast.

If children find it hard to share something with parents, it would be most helpful for them to be able to share with some other adult. Oftentimes children share with their peers, who may not be able to present a broader view based on wider experience.

A mother recently discovered that her nineteen year old son was gay. After the shock, she gained additional information, discovering that he knew of his homosexual orientation since he was eleven years old. She was deeply touched by the realization that her son had carried this awareness within himself for eight years without being able to share it with any adult. How good it would have been if this child could have opened up this area of his young life with his parents or with an understanding adult friend or relative.

5. Children's Masturbation

Right from the start I would like to caution you, as parents, to react slowly and calmly to your children's masturbation. Quick, negative reactions speak a million words and tend to push this area of sexuality into secrecy.

First of all, I suggest that you attend to your own beliefs and values regarding masturbation. Most of us in the Judaeo-Christian tradition have been raised shrouding all areas of sexuality in guilt and shame. Consequently, our emotional responses to sex probably tend to come from those earlier influences, even though intellectually we might believe less dramatically today about the evils of masturbation. By attending to our emotional responses, we can learn to modify and control them when dealing with our children in the area of sexuality.

Secondly, it will help to see childhood masturbation as a signal of something else rather than an event with significance in itself. Masturbation, like crying or laughing, tells us that something is moving more deeply within the child. "What is it?" should be our parental pursuit, not "How awful!"

A child might have a bored body. He sits around watching TV all Saturday morning, and since he has nothing else to do he plays with his penis and discovers masturbation. Or after school, the young girl listens to her turned up stereo and ends up massaging her clitoris to orgasm. These are kids with bored bodies. As parents, I think you would do well to focus on the boredom, not the masturbation. If the kids were out playing in the snow they would be stimulating their bodies in a more fully energized way.

Masturbation may be signaling a number of other things too. The child might be curious and exploring his or her body. In dealing with the child you then focus on the curiosity. A child may be lonely. Then focus on that. A child may seek all kinds of pleasures impulsively without considering all the consequences. You focus on that. A child may simply have discovered a physical source of pleasure. You attend to his or her seeking pleasure.

In other words, I do not think that attempting to place a lot of moral right or wrong on masturbation itself helps a child to understand and integrate his or her sexual dynamic. It is better, I believe, to focus on what the sexual activity signifies, and attend to that.

Remember what you are working toward: sex is most rich and rewarding in the context of love. When children's sexual behavior begins to signal a strong self-centered egotistic orientation, then your concern may be justified: not because of the sexual activity itself, but because of the powerful inward orientation. Such an orientation leads a child away from the ability to love. That's the problem. We want the child to grow in his or her power of loving. Then, you see, sex will be well-integrated in the child's life.

Finally, you need to talk with your children when you discover them masturbating, just as you would if they were eating candy before supper every day. Talk with them, not so much as a problem to be solved, but to place the activity in the context of a full human life.

Start by receiving the child, then make a little input. For example: "Paul, I know that playing with your penis must give you some physical pleasure. That's called a sexual act. And sex is something pretty special that is meant mostly as a true expression of love between two people. I know that young people often are curious about their bodies and want to know how they work. And that's fine. As you do find out more about your body, I'd like you to keep in mind what I said, that sex is best used and most complete when it happens between a man and a woman who truly love each other and have committed themselves to each other."

What you should try to do is always place sex in the context of love. If you keep that in mind, you will teach your children well about their sexuality.

Chapter 12

The Skill of Loving and
Contemplating

Love and contemplation both involve the act of union. Love is one person's union with another person, while contemplation is one person's union with a non-personal aspect of creation. The dynamic is similar; the object of the union is different.

Skill of Loving

One of the most fulfilling and enriching dimensions of human life is the experience of true intimacy and love. Many adults fear and avoid close interpersonal relationships, oftentimes due to childhood experiences. Perhaps here more than any other area of child development, the best way of teaching is to model and give love.

Love cannot be taught. It needs to be experienced by children. But you can do a few things to help them experience and become comfortable with love.

First of all, you can express your love for the children. The bumper sticker "Have you hugged your kids today?" may not say it all, but it does highlight the importance of physical and verbal statements of love. I realize that some parents and teachers are not expressive people and find it uncomfortable to share warm feelings with their children. I encourage you to work to overcome your inhibition and discomfort and to say those magic words: "I love you." If that seems too difficult at first, try statements like: "I think you're a neat kid; I really enjoyed going to the game with you; I sure like you."

Starting when your children are very small will make it easier. They will simply grow up surrounded by those expressions of love and learn to give them back to you easily. That, too, will make it easier for you. From the beginning, before our children could even understand words, we told them often about our love for them. When each child reached the age of two and a half years, they began saying back to us: "I love you, too." Then one night my son said to me: "Good night, Dad. See you in the morning. I love you more than any Dad in the whole world." He has said that ever since. His younger sister now says the same thing. He modeled for her a way of expressing love. Their expressions of love have made it easier for us to declare our love to them. The demonstration of love is contagious. It spreads. We as parents only planted the seeds.

The second thing we can do is express our love to our marriage partner or to other adults in the presence of the children. The kids may tease us and poke fun, but they learn a comfort with expressing affection if they see adults at ease with it.

Third, we can help our children learn love by revealing our own needs and invite them to minister to them (from Chapter 5). As I wrote earlier, children tend to be focused inwardly. They respond to their own needs and desires more easily than to those of others. By speaking to our children about our own feelings, thoughts, and needs, we invite them to attend to us and not just to themselves. By stating *your* problem with their behavior we call them to respond to our need. They may not always do so, but at least we are presenting them with the choice. When they do respond, they are loving us in a practical and concrete way.

Finally, we can help our children learn love by creating a cooperative rather than antagonistic relationship between ourself and our spouse. When a couple works together in a family unit, love pervades that family setting. The couple is sensitive to each other's needs, responds to the other's concerns; the couple enjoys each other, does things together, takes leisure together, and works together so both parties come out winners. The couple forms a real partnership. And that partnership includes the children.

But if the marriage relationship moves in an antagonistic way, then competitiveness rather than love fills the family situation. Each parent tries to protect self against the other, and so does not often attend to the other's need. Because they stand apart from each other—against each other—they cannot form a partnership. They are in a contest against each other, trying to gain their own victories. Such a dynamic, of course, cannot teach love to children.

Consequently, if you want to teach your children the skill of loving, it might be instructive to check your marriage relationship. If it is cooperative, you are in the process of teaching love to your children. If you discover a competitive or antagonistic flavor to the relationship, you are teaching your children how to take care of themselves and protect against the needs and desires of others. In a cooperative marriage both partners and each child come out winners. In an antagonistic relationship, partners are trying to win and cause the other to lose. What actually happens, however, is that both parents and every child end up a loser. Love cannot thrive in a situation which creates losers.

Skill of Contemplation

This skill may sound a little foreign to you. Perhaps you haven't thought of contemplation as a skill useful to your child. However, it appears that lifeful persons display the ability to contemplate.

Contemplation flows out of the skill of loving. To love someone means to become united with that person in a positive, life-giving way. Love happens between two persons. Contemplation is also a union that leads to a positive, life-giving conclusion. But the union is formed between a person and a non-person.

To contemplate means to observe, or notice, or attend to with your mind and feelings. When you observe the sunset and allow yourself to enter it as fully as possible you contemplate. You become momentarily united with the sun in a positive, life-giving way. Contemplation is a result of the skill of engagement, whereby you actively enter into a union with another piece of reality and enjoy the experience.

In some respects, children seem to possess some natural ability to contemplate. However, as parents and teachers you can help that skill to develop. Certainly, nature is the best place to teach contemplation. You can set up all sorts of situations in which your children can enter into and observe the richness of nature. As I sit in my den on a bright autumn morning before anyone else is awake, I realize that my children have never seen a sunrise. Soon it might be fun to have a sunrise party. We can watch the sun come up, marvel at it, jog around the park connected to our backyard, and then go out to breakfast together. (After that, their Mom and I might need to go back to bed for a bit.)

We could observe the leaves on the trees turning colors; we could look inside the shrubs to see what's there; we could find the bugs and see how they are getting ready for winter, etc. Creating these experiences for your children depends on your ability to take a little time and observe things yourselves. To help your children contemplate calls for a little energy from you and some noticing of the life around you. Then your job is simply to point it out to your children—and to let yourselves *enjoy* what you point out. Your enjoyment excites and calls your children to become united with the reality you are observing. That is contemplation, a positive and life-giving union with the world around you.

I prefer not to write much more about the skills of love and contemplation because they stand, in part, as the fruits of the other skills. If children develop their ability to believe in their own goodness, to give and receive in communication with each other, to believe realistically about the world they live in, and to engage their reality fully, they will grow into loving and contemplative people. They will seek bondedness with each other as persons in union with all the enriching aspects of creation. Love and contemplation stand as the finest expression of the fully human person.

Skills for the Parents-Teachers

Chapter 13

Making the Transition
from Authority to Consultant

To help children develop their life skills, parents and teachers need to make an important transition in their relationship to the children. We can understand this transition best by seeing the stages of parenting. Just as children pass through various stages of growth, so, too, do parents (and to a lesser degree teachers) have stages to work through.

Sometimes these stages seem easy and natural; at other times they feel labored and painful. When parents match their development to that of their children, then they can best teach their youngsters life skills.

Four different stages or roles surface in the lives of parents corresponding to four stages of children's growth.

Nurturer

First, parents function as nurturers, caring for their newborn child's every need. In a state of sheer *dependence*, the child elicits in us that warm and tender dimension known as motherly or fatherly love. We change baby's diapers, feed, clothe, cuddle, bounce baby on the knee and carry the child everywhere. Nurturing rises up in us naturally. We don't have to work at it. As long as the child is totally dependent, we function solely as nurturers.

Authority

But very shortly baby begins asserting himself or herself. At around seven months Tommy begins to creep—this inaugu-

rates stage two for the child—*testing the limits.* Role two also
begins for the parent-authority. Parental authority surfaces out
of the nurturing role as a form of protecting the child from
harm. The parent attempts to keep Tommy safe and does so by
setting the limits in which he can navigate.

As soon as Tommy begins to explore, Dad and Mom start
using their authority. They set up gates at the stairs; they say
no when he pokes the dog; they take away the plastic bag he's
playing with; they slap his fingers when he tries sticking them
in the electrical outlet. All these authoritative moves are for the
child's welfare.

As Tommy gets older his parents continue using authority
for the child's safety. They insist: "You cannot cross the busy
street"; "You must get to bed by seven"; "You must eat all your
food."

At this point, the waters become slightly muddy. Parents
can also begin to use authority for reasons other than the child's
safety. They can use their authoritative power for their own
gratification and the satisfaction of their own needs. Children's
yelling while Mom talks on the phone may be a time she uses
authority to quiet the kids, not for their safety, but for her sanity. The same occurs when Dad insists that a teenager turn down
the radio. He does that for his sake.

These two motives for parental authority—the child's
safety and the gratification of parents' needs—get mixed
together in daily family life. The effect on children of this mix is
confusion. Children find it difficult to interpret their parents'
authority as an act of concern. They often view it as aggression
or as the parents' selfish needs to have things their way.

I believe, then, that the reason children have such difficulty
with parental authority is that they do not see it as an act of
loving concern on the parents' part. They don't see it because
parents have used authority to gain their own satisfaction as
well as for the children's well-being.

Generally, I believe that parental authority is appropriately
used when looking out for the child's safety. We need to set lim-

its to protect our children's well-being. But authority used to gain our gratification as parents needs careful discernment. I encourage you not to use your authority to gain your needs unless all other avenues have been closed. And when you do use authority in these instances you should use it in a respectful and careful way.

If you have attempted to gain your children's cooperation regarding a need you have, and they have refused to respond to your need, then you may have to use authority. But can you use the authority to help the children learn how to cooperate rather than as a tool for the satisfaction of your needs? In other words, can you use it for *their* sake, their growth, rather than as a way of getting what you want?

To be used in a human, growing way, authority must be seen to help the child protect himself or herself physically and psychologically. Its purpose is to aid the child in developing a way of thinking and acting that will help him or her grow personally and interpersonally. Certainly as parents we have the role of creating rules based on acceptable norms of life. But those rules should always consider, first of all, the child's development as a person, not our gratification as a parent.

For instance, if Laura is making a lot of noise while mother talks on the phone, authority should be employed to help her learn appropriate cooperative behavior. This can be accomplished by setting the limits of what Laura can and cannot do when someone is talking on the phone. If she stays within those limits she will experience the social rewards of life in this family. If she steps beyond those limits she will experience the consequences of inappropriate behavior—in this case, perhaps sitting in a corner chair until Mom is finished with the phone conversation. Thus, Laura learns how to become responsible for her behavior. (Much more of this notion was explored in Chapter 7.)

Thus, children's major difficulty with parental authority develops because they often interpret all forms of authoritative action as oppressive rather than loving. If parents use authority to gratify their own needs, or if they use authority in a strong-armed, verbally or physically violent manner, their children will misinterpret the parents' loving concern for them. This misunderstanding is painful for me to see in a family. The parents love the children; the children love the parents. But the manner in which the parents use authority often drives ever deeper wedges between themselves and their children. As you continue reading, you will see some ways to use authority so that it does not fracture the family relationships.

Consultant

When children begin to *think independently* their parents are called to role three—consultants. The transition from authority to consultant stands as one of the most difficult tasks we have as parents. The consultant has three functions:

1. To gather as much information from the client as possible (for a parent or teacher this means primarily listening effectively).
2. To give information (not mere opinion) about the situation.
3. Based on that information, to make recommendations about what to do.

The consultant stands *with* the client and helps the client discover his or her own solution based on data and reason. Certainly young children are not always fully capable of using data and reason in deciding their actions. But, by gradually working in that direction, you, as parents, aid them in becoming independent and sensible thinkers and doers. If you over-use authority with your children, you will cut off their opportunities to learn independent thinking. You teach them that their ideas and positions are not worth much. By being overly authoritative, children learn precisely what you probably don't want them to learn—they learn to accept other people's opinions and choices and not make their own. Most parents I talk with want their children to be independent thinkers. They don't want them to succumb to "peer pressure." <u>Your best chance of reaching that goal with your children is to shift more and more from an authoritative to a consultative role.</u>

I would like to highlight for you the difference between an authoritative and consultative style of parenting. <u>The authority reacts *very quickly* to events. Parents in this mold *remain in their own world* with their views and judgments.</u> They rarely listen effectively to their children. They are certain of the rightness of their ways, which makes them quite inflexible.

<u>Consultants, on the other hand, *slow down* their internal processes and first try to understand their child and the situation. They *leave their world* and judgments for a while to enter the world of the child. Then they try to assess the situation with the child and make recommendations about what to do.</u>

Recently, a mother told me of her fourteen year old son and how one day she discovered marijuana in his bedroom. A purely authoritative parent would have immediately destroyed the pot, severely reprimanded the boy, insisting that he never again smoke the stuff, and then punish him by grounding for a month.

This mother operated more as a consultant. She was upset when she discovered it. But then she recovered and calmed herself before approaching her son and said, "Tim, I think it's important for us to talk about the pot I found in your room this morning." They talked for a half hour, with Mom simply trying to understand her son. After she felt she knew what *his* position was, she attempted to give him some information on pot and her own beliefs about it. Then she said: "I know I can't stop you from smoking if you really insist on it, but I sure think you should find out as much about it as possible and quit because I can't see it doing you any good."

That was Mom, the pure consultant. With adults, pure consultation oftentimes works effectively. But with children, parents usually need to mix consultation and authority to get the best results.

In the above example, Mother blended these two roles well. A week after the incident she asked Tim what he'd done about the pot and he gave a vague answer. Since Mom did not have much information about pot herself, and since Tim wasn't doing anything on his own, she told him she would look for a program on drugs and drug abuse for Tim to attend. She discovered a six session series on drug abuse for parents and teens and asked Tim to go with her. He refused and she insisted (authority role). After each session they discussed it (consultant role). She told Tim that he could not smoke or have pot in the house (authority role), but although she disapproved and hoped he would stop entirely, she knew the choice was his and that outside her presence she had no power to stop him (consultant role).

As our children become teenagers our role as consultants becomes much more important. If we continue to operate out of an authoritative style (role two) while they are functioning in stage three—independent thinker and doer—we run the risk of losing a significant and influencing relationship with them. They have already established, or are in the process of establishing, many values and beliefs about themselves and the world around them. During this time we want to have influence in the formation of those values, but that influence cannot come by functioning as authorities. We cannot legislate our children's values. It is like demanding that a tree grow three inches a year with eighteen new branches each season.

All we can do as authoritative parents is to control our children's *behavior* as long as they are in our presence. In fact, our use of authority can have the opposite effect. The greater the force we exert as parents, the greater the resistance from our children. This finding, given to us by social psychologists, might help us give up a strong authoritative role for a more consultative role. Strong authority with children who are learning independence simply does not work.

Certain areas of teenage life literally defy parental authority. The major conflict areas all involve values—they include drugs, drinking, friends, religion, sex, and school work. These tend to stand as the difficult spots between parents and teens. I would strongly recommend that in dealing with these issues you try to serve as consultants rather than authorities. The authoritative position cannot work—it does not change the children's values, but may reinforce them instead. Authority may impede their behavior slightly (although I doubt it), but it drives children away from their parents. Then if the children do get into serious difficulty in any of these sensitive areas, they will not come to an authoritative parent, whose reaction will only be more authoritative.

The consulting style offers the opportunity for continued dialogue and reasonable thinking and openness while a child searches for what is best for him or her. The child may still decide against your belief, but you may well save the relationship. And I do not believe that any issue is big enough to destroy the open and caring relationship between parent and child.

Friend

Finally, we arrive at the role of friend. This usually occurs when the child leaves the home and has gained social and financial independence. Once parents experience the end of full responsibility for the child, a deeper friendship then develops. This role for the parent corresponds to the child's fourth stage of development—*inter-dependence*. Here the young adult has experienced independent living and thinking, and now recognizes his or her need for others. The child reaches out now in a more mature giving and receiving type of relationship, the stuff of which true friendships are made.

In discussing these various roles of parental development, I do not want to suggest that you cannot be friends to your children while they live with you. No, these various roles only take a more prominent place at different times of life. Again, the most difficult of transitions from one role to another is between the authority and consultant roles. Making that shift will not only improve your relationships with your children, but will give you considerably more influence in the formation of their values and beliefs, and help you teach them the skills discussed throughout this book.

Summary of Parent and Child Development

Parent   **Child**
            Matches

1. Nurturer   1. Totally dependent
2. Authority   2. Exploring and testing limits
3. Consultant   3. Striving for independence
4. Friend   4. Becoming inter-dependent

Chapter 14

Managing Feelings and Behaviors

The educational process works best when the teachers or parents have control over their feelings and behaviors. Oftentimes, in working with children, our feelings and behaviors can have control over us.

What feelings and behaviors do you have as a parent or teacher that you would like to change? Do you wish that you were not so impatient, did not get so angry, did not worry so much, did not feel so hurt when the kids forgot about you? Do you wish that you could stop nagging so much, quit yelling when you talk to the kids, be more attentive to them when they talk with you, or give up spanking or hitting as a common response to misbehavior?

I want to show you a way to modify your feelings and behaviors. But it will take work on your part. Just reading the chapter will not do it. What I say here will make a lot of sense to you. You will probably want to try this process out. When you do, you may discover that it does not seem to work. Then you might be tempted to say, "Well, that was a nice theory, but it doesn't work in real life." With this statement, it will become simple to go back to yelling. At least, you think, yelling gets the upset out of your system.

I do not want that to sound like a self-fulfilling prophecy. You *can* change your feelings and behavior, but one or two efforts to change a response pattern that has developed over a number of years is like trying to chop down a tree with a dinner knife. You are trying to break a habit, and habits do not give up easily. So, if you want to change certain feelings and behaviors, you need to really want to change and you need to keep working hard on breaking the old pattern.

To make the changes you desire, it is helpful to understand how your feelings and behaviors are created. Many people believe that emotions are caused from outside ourselves. You may say, "Those kids make me so mad," or "They drive me crazy sometimes," or "They make me very proud." We place the cause of our emotions in our children, believing that they have the power to make us happy or sad, anxious or calm. When we were little, we believed that outside forces made us react in certain ways, and that we had no inner control over our responses. We believed that the reason we hit our sister was because she hit us first; that we could not "help it" when we got in a fight because our brother "started it." Every time he did a nasty little trick, comedian Flip Wilson would say, "The devil made me do it." As children, we held the magical belief that forces outside ourselves controlled our behavior and feelings.

Recently, I watched a five year old boy standing at the curb of the street as a large dump truck rumbled by. He made a hand motion to the driver to beep his horn. The driver honked a couple of times. The boy ran excitedly to his father, claiming, "I made the truck driver beep his horn." That is a child's magical belief regarding the cause of emotions and behaviors.

The *first step* in modifying your emotions and behaviors, then, lies in realizing that *you* create your own feelings and behaviors. They are not caused from outside yourself. Your children do not make you angry or drive you up a wall or bug you. You and I do those things to ourselves. Certainly, the kids need to be there goofing around, etc., but you cause your own responses to them. If the cause of your emotions resided in your children, then you and your spouse should react in the same way every time the children did the same things. But you both respond differently to the same stimulus, and in fact you respond differently yourself at different times.

Once you realize that you create your feelings—you make yourself angry, impatient, worried, sad, happy, proud, violent— then you have the power to change your feelings and behaviors.

Only when you realize that the power for change lies within you can you take charge of altering your actions and feelings.

More accurately, then, you might express your responses this way:

"I really upset myself when the kids fight."
"I do so much worrying when Susan is late."
"I make myself so impatient when the children don't come right away."
"I feel hurt when he says that."

rather than this way:

"They make me so mad when they fight."
"She worries me sick."
"They drive me up the wall when they don't come right away."
"He hurt my feelings."

Step two in the process of changing your feelings has to do with understanding how your sabotaging feelings are created and maintained. Psychologist Albert Ellis is helpful here. He, along with a growing number of therapists and professionals, believes that your feelings are created, not by the event outside yourself, but by the way you *think* about the event. Your thinking generates your feelings and behaviors. What you think and believe will determine the kind and intensity of your feelings.

For example, when your teenage daughter fails to come home at 11:00 P.M., her curfew time, you will experience different feelings depending on how you are thinking.

You might feel . . .	*because you think . . .*
1. anger	1. she should be, must be home on time. She's disobedient.
2. worry	2. she was probably in a car accident; or maybe she was raped.

You might feel . . .	*because you think . . .*
3. disappointment	3. she broke our agreement; I can't trust her anymore.
4. revenge	4. well, I'll be damned if I'm going to let her out again at night. After all I did for her, and she can't even follow this one rule.

As you can see, what you *think* will determine your feelings.

The key, then, to modifying your feelings lies in attending to your thoughts and beliefs. Ellis presents this in the following way:

A. Activating Event—Daughter out past curfew.

B. Beliefs and Thoughts about A.

C. Leading to the Consequences, namely your emotions and behaviors.

B, your thoughts, create your feelings. Often this is referred to as "self-talk."

Step three involves checking over your thinking process to make sure your thoughts and beliefs match reality. Just because you and I believe something to be true does not make it so. Many of our beliefs never get challenged, and so remain operating in us. We believe our thoughts to be reasonable and sensible; if they were not, we would throw them out of our thinking. But simply because we believe does not make reality that way.

We possess, in fact, two kinds of beliefs: rational and irrational. Rational beliefs are based on reality; they are consistent with the way things actually are; they lead to happiness and well-being. Irrational beliefs, on the other hand, are based on fabrications of our mind or the minds of others; they have no contact with the real world, and are fundamentally nonsensical;

they lead to sabotaging emotions, such as anger, depression and worry.

As parents, we have a variety of thoughts that are irrational and create sabotaging and debilitating feelings and behaviors. In Chapter 6 I outlined certain irrational beliefs of children. Some of those can also be found in parents and teachers.

1. Catastrophic or Dramatic Thoughts

As parents or educators, we can look at a situation and then blow it up bigger than life with dramatic thinking. We say, "Isn't this awful," "I can't stand it anymore," "They are driving me crazy," "I feel just devastated," "I am worried to death."

When your son does not come home on time you might dramatize, "His car is in a ditch and he's bleeding to death." When your young daughter says, "I hate you," you might think catastrophically, "Oh my God, my daughter has no love for me anymore."

Dramatic thinking pops up in parents most easily when we feel stress. Then we make grand and sweeping statements such as: "You never do anything around here," "You're always goofing off," "I've never seen anyone as sloppy as you," "I can't believe anyone could do something so dumb."

Considerable drama weaves throughout our thought patterns. Generally, it does not accurately express reality. It inflates it, pumping it up larger than what is warranted. Then we respond to that non-realistic world. If we can modify the drama within us, we will tone down our emotional responses to daily living.

Watch for your dramatic thinking in the small details of life. I found myself getting impatient every night at the children's bedtime. They "took forever" getting ready for bed. It seemed as though my son "took an hour" to get his shoes off and my daughter spent an "eternity" putting on her pajamas. I began snapping at them, so that by the time they finally got into bed I was angry and they were upset. Anyone would become angry, you see, if they believed they were spending "eternity" putting their children to bed.

Once I noticed my dramatic thinking, I began talking to myself more reasonably. I said, "Wait a second, Dale! This is not taking forever. In the great scheme of life's events, it is taking about five minutes longer. That's all. Why not let your children live these five minutes casually and gracefully." I am better now at their bedtime. Certainly, I continue to keep moving them along, but I do not have the impatience and upset I experienced before. Five minutes is no longer "forever."

Catastrophic and dramatic thoughts serve to intensify any reaction we have to a situation. By making those thoughts more modest and accurate, we defuse many emotions and behaviors and function in a more calm and graceful way.

2. Demand Thoughts

More than any other set of irrational thoughts, demand thinking gets us, as parents, into serious trouble. Karen Horney has talked of these thoughts as "the tyranny of the shoulds." If you understand the irrationality of demand thoughts, you will go a long way in significantly reducing your angers.

We make a demand thought every time we say in our mind, "should, must, ought to, has to, absolutely, necessary, no other way, etc." We demand that reality fit our prescription for it. Each of us possesses tremendous legislative power. We make up rules for all kinds of situations, from the way other drivers should drive, to the way our child cuts his hair. But while we have this legislative power, we rarely possess executive power to enforce our rules for the world. You can see how inherently frustrating that is. How would you like to be elected a Senator, go to Washington and pass laws, only to have the executive branch say it can't or won't enforce that law? You would become frustrated—the stepping stone to anger.

But, you might be wondering, what is irrational about wanting things a certain way? First of all, if you do not have executive power (that is, if you are helpless in gaining your demand), to continue to insist within yourself that A should be C is nonsensical. Reality does not change just because inside yourself you demand it to be other than the way it is. To insist within yourself that your children not fight with each other does not stop them from fighting. The reality is that they are, in fact, fighting. Now, you may not like that and want it to change, but to be insisting within yourself that they must not be fighting only frustrates and upsets you. The fact is that they are fighting. Your inner insistence that they not fight, and your subsequent upset, do not, in the long run, reduce the amount of fighting. Your upset, in other words, does not help you or your children. It only complicates the problem before you, namely their fighting.

Problem number one is the children fighting. Problem number two is your anger. When you bring problem two along to deal with problem one you seriously complicate the matter. Now you are trying to get the children to stop fighting while you are angry. By taking out the "shoulds" regarding children fighting, you effectively undercut your anger, and you can now deal with problem one without intense upset because your shoulds did not interfere. The reality is simply that the children do fight. You do not like it. How can you intelligently and reasonably get them to stop now and in the future? If you free yourself from the "shoulds," you will be able to turn to discipline by action (Chapter 7) without undue anger and upset.

One of the most irrational shoulds of parents comes up almost every evening at suppertime. When you call the children to supper, they probably do not come on the first call. Eight calls later they arrive. The irrational belief that leads to your eventual irritation and upset sounds like this: "My children should come to the table the first time they are called." That may sound reasonable to you, but it flies in the face of reality almost daily. Children never have and probably never will come on the first call. So why do we go on insisting within ourselves that they must come immediately? We only upset ourselves, and make our mealtime miserable.

It is more reasonable to acknowledge that young children will be drawn to Sesame Street before asparagus tips, and older children would rather continue their phone conversation than eat liver and onions. That's reality. There are no shoulds about it. Kids are the way they are. Now, again, if you do not like it that way, you can work to change it, but upsetting yourself by internal demands does not get your children to the table on the first call. Free from inner shoulds, you will be liberated from your anger. And free from anger, you can create more effective behavior strategies to get your children to the table after calling only once (Chapter 7).

When you notice the "shoulds" popping up in your thinking, you want to try changing the *demand* quality of that inner statement to a *desire*. "My child must not use foul language" can be altered to *wishing* he would not, and then working calmly toward achieving that end.

An existential point of view helps here. What exists, exists. If we knew all the occurrences in the life of this child, his or her thoughts and beliefs, we would almost never say "should" or "must not." We would only say, "It makes sense that he or she is acting this way." We may not like the way that our children are responding, but it does make sense when you lay out their life's history and the full pattern of their beliefs. Our children are the way they are ... for good reasons. Calling them calmly to change and grow certainly beats *demanding* that they change in the midst of upset and anger.

3. Blame Statements

Thoughts of blame and accusation almost always lead to depression (if directed toward self) or to anger (if directed toward our children). They are fundamentally irrational, because they involve sweeping judgments about the whole person based on an external behavior. In Chapter 2 I talked of making statements about your children according to their behavior. Calling a child "stupid" because he or she made a poor judgment regarding some event is an irrational and nonsensical thought that leads to your upset and a put-down to the child.

In this chapter I want to focus on the blame statements you might be making about yourself as a parent or a teacher. Due to the unpredictability of children's development and to the lack of preparation in assuming the parental role, most of us begin our parenting careers from a position of inadequacy. We oftentimes start out very young in life assuming this great responsibility.

We may be facing a series of other serious issues of life when we become parents, ranging from our marriage relationship to job to money to loss of long-time, single, school friends.

All of a sudden we become parents. We may not have paid much attention to the course we had in high school on family life. It did not apply at the time. So we begin our parental life not too sure of what we are doing.

With a set of question marks and uncertainty as a backdrop, we plunge into our new role. When the baby cries often, we can easily begin inferring that something might be wrong with us. "Maybe I'm doing something wrong." "Perhaps, I'm messing up this little child's life." In other words, if we start out not being sure of ourselves, then when the child reacts in a negative way, it is easy to draw conclusions about ourselves as parents.

Once that process gets going, you can develop a thinking habit that blames yourself whenever your children act in unusual or uncommon ways. You will then become depressed and beat yourself up. At this point, you can get caught in a vicious circle, since once you become depressed, you will more likely react negatively to your children, and they to you. This will lead to further blame of self, more depression, and even more negative reactions to yourself and your children.

Most of you, I suspect, can see the unreality of making a universal statement about another person based on his or her behavior. If Danny yells at times (even often) he is not, therefore, a "brat." He is a boy who yells a lot. But when it comes to self, it may be more difficult to see that you are not "an inadequate mother" because you seem too impatient with the children.

Working with parents in therapy, I find it difficult for them to break that self-blame pattern. "What did we do wrong?" they ask. I believe they assume that the child's difficulty is their (the parents') external forces that have touched this child's life. Somehow they believe that theirs was the only influence in the child's history. Consequently, when the child runs into difficulty, the parents wonder what they did wrong as parents.

Recently, a mother of two small girls came to me depressed. She complained: "I am such an awful mother. I yell at the kids. I even hit Ann yesterday. I hardly ever do that. I don't know what's the matter with me. I should never have had the children. I am ruining their lives."

What havoc this thinking had on this mother. If you believed you were destroying the children you loved, you would become depressed, too, and draw her conclusion: "Therefore, I am no good as a parent." But wait. If she were no good, she wouldn't get depressed. She's depressed precisely because she *loves* those kids. If she did not love them, she would not care what was happening to them. So, in fact, she is a loving mother (great) who yells at her children. Okay. She can work on the yelling, but she needs to hold on to the awareness of her love for them. With the awareness of a deep love for her children, it becomes harder for her to conclude, "And, therefore, I am inadequate."

A parent resents the great amount of time the children demand. Mothers generally experience this more than fathers. A mother may find herself resisting doing what the children want. She has not had any time for herself, and would just like a few minutes or an hour to get some work done. But those children are present like ants around sugar. She feels like screaming. She has had it. She wants to walk out. She wishes she had never had kids. She never bargained for this trip.

Almost simultaneously with her feelings of resentment and resistance toward her children, this mom begins feeling guilty. She says to herself: "What kind of a mother am I anyway? How can I have these awful feelings? I'm not fit to be a mother. I must really be terrible." Of course, she now ends up depressed as well as resentful. Her depression does not help her. Rather, it drives her further into a hole. Her guilt and blame serve to depress her. Her thoughts about herself are basically irrational and out of touch with reality.

She certainly does not become a "bad mom" if she feels resistant and resentful toward her children. If that were true, perhaps the majority of parents would have to be labeled "bad." To help herself, Mom needs to think more sensibly. For example,

"Yes, I am feeling resistant and resentful toward these children. I seem to have very little personal space in my life at this time, and I need some. I acknowledge my feelings, and accept them as signals to me of something more important moving within my heart."

You see, Mom does not allow herself to:

1. Make a broad sweeping statement about herself based on a feeling. She sees the feeling as a signal of something deep within.
2. Make any moral judgment about her feeling. It is not right or wrong. It is simply there.

Now, she takes a minute to get in touch with the deep energy within her signaled by her resentment. What does it really mean? What do I really seek? She discovers that, deep within her, she moves toward a sense of freedom. She feels the need for aloneness, time and space simply to relax and be her own self— not Mom, not feeder, clother, provider, understanding shoulder. She needs to be her own person for a little while.

She recognizes that energy and says: "That's normal and okay. I can embrace that about me. I am one who needs moments simply to be me and not play all these demanding, nurturing roles. I am not a bad mother because I get resentful. I am a good, normal person who wants to be whole, and at times that gets expressed as resentment. Okay, I accept myself as I am."

So, rather than blame yourself as an inadequate parent based on your feelings and behavior, use those external reactions as signals of deep, rich energies moving within you toward fulfillment, freedom and love. Try to separate your feelings and behaviors from your identity as a person or a parent. You are not your feelings or your behaviors. Those things emanate from you, but are not you. Rather, you are your inner drives and energies. And these deep movements are totally good. To avoid self-blame, then, you will want to focus on these deep energies and ask how they can be directly expressed and fulfilled; you will not want to focus simply on your external feelings and behaviors as the determiners of your adequacy.

Let me summarize, then, the steps in dealing effectively with your feelings, especially those you want to change.

1. An event takes place.
2. You immediately state a set of thoughts and beliefs about the event, some of which are rational, others being irrational.
3. Based primarily on the irrational beliefs, you experience a sabotaging feeling.
4. To change the feeling, you try to dispute your *thinking* that leads to the feeling.
5. You continue practicing your new thinking, challenging your old catastrophic, or demand, or blame statements.
6. Gradually, as you learn to think in a new, more realistic way, your old thoughts begin to break up, and your old sabotaging feelings begin to leave you.

This process takes perseverance. Do not give up once you start. Your old thought habits die hard. You are addicted to these patterns just as an alcoholic is addicted to liquor. If you want to change your feelings, you will need to fight as strongly as the alcoholic or drug addict. Like them, you will succeed if you stick with it taking it one hour at a time (I can avoid irrational thinking for this hour), and forcing yourself to stay away from as much nonsensical believing as possible.

Chapter 15

Modeling a Full Human Life

No doubt it has been evident throughout this book that our best approach to teaching children life skills is our own modeling. The do-as-I-say, not-as-I-do approach never did work. Children learn the skills that parents and teachers practice best. Of course, we need not possess all these skills totally in order to teach them, but it helps if we are consciously developing the skills ourselves.

Children gain a sense of the rich human life from the fullness of our own human living. If they experience the spirit of love and unity, and oftentimes joy, that exudes from us as the result of our humanness, they will seek to do what we do to gain such a sense of well-being. If, on the other hand, they see hostility, depression and pessimism shrouding us, they will hardly model the skills we present. Much less likely will they attend to our words of advice about how to live life.

Despite all the "how-to" books for parents and teachers, the fundamental teaching device remains your *person*. You are the message. If you like who you are, your children have a better chance of liking who they are. If you listen well, so will your kids (generally). If you are self-revealing, they will be comfortable with the expression of feeling. If you engage the world as it is, most likely they will, too. And so it goes.

By your life, then, *you* teach children life skills. Those skills discussed in this book apply equally to you as adults as they do to your children. If you want to attain a rich, full life, these are the skills needed. The more you grow in them personally, the richer you will be. Your children's inheritance, then, will be your full life developed through and expressed by the life skills.